The Heart and Law of Islam: A Journey Through Fiqh and Aqeedah

MAA

Published by MAA, 2025.

THE HEART AND LAW OF ISLAM: A JOURNEY THROUGH FIQH AND AQEEDAH

First edition. June 10, 2025.

ISBN: 979-8231632947

Written by MAA.

Chapter 1: The Primordial Covenant — Belief in Allah Since Creation

Long before the first human soul took its first breath on earth, a covenant was made—silent in memory but etched into the essence of every human being. It is known in the Islamic tradition as **al-Mithaq**, the **Primordial Covenant**, and it signifies the earliest moment of conscious recognition between Creator and creation.

1. The Quranic Account of the Covenant

The foundation of this concept is found in the Quran, specifically in Surah Al-A'raf (7:172):

> *"And [mention] when your Lord took from the children of Adam—from their loins—their descendants and made them testify concerning themselves, [saying to them], 'Am I not your Lord?' They said, 'Yes, we have testified.' [This]—lest you should say on the Day of Resurrection, 'Indeed, we were unaware of this.'"*

This verse outlines a metaphysical event: the progeny of Adam, extracted from his spine in a realm unknown to this world, testified to Allah's Lordship. This moment, though unremembered in the conscious mind, defines the spiritual identity of every human being. According to numerous scholars, including Ibn Abbas and Mujahid, this verse is not metaphorical but refers to a real event in the pre-earthly realm.

2. The Nature of Fitrah: Innate Disposition

Islamic theology places great importance on the concept of **fitrah**—the natural, God-given inclination to recognize and worship Allah. The Prophet Muhammad (pbuh) said:

> *"Every child is born upon the fitrah (natural disposition). Then his parents make him a Jew, or a Christian, or a Magian..."* (Sahih al-Bukhari and Muslim)

This statement illustrates that the knowledge of God is not an external construct acquired by culture or reasoning, but an inner recognition present from birth. The Primordial Covenant is thus not simply a legal declaration but an embedded awareness, which becomes clouded—not erased—by environment and experience.

3. The Implication of Responsibility

By making all of humanity testify to His Lordship, Allah eliminated the possibility of ignorance as an excuse. The Qur'anic rationale is precise: *"lest you should say on the Day of Resurrection, 'We were unaware of this.'"* The burden of recognition and obedience does not begin with earthly life; it is inherited from a commitment made before time itself. This belief serves as a foundation for human accountability in Islamic doctrine.

4. The Covenant Across Nations

The notion of a shared recognition of God is not limited to Muslims. The Quran repeatedly references past nations—'Ad, Thamud, Bani Israel—who were sent messengers because they possessed the same primordial awareness. Surah Al-Nahl (16:36) affirms:

> *"And We certainly sent into every nation a messenger, [saying], 'Worship Allah and avoid Taghut (false gods).'"*

This indicates that the knowledge of God is universal, and messengers were sent not to introduce a new God, but to remind nations of the One they had already testified to.

5. Philosophical and Theological Interpretations

Islamic theologians have interpreted al-Mithaq in various ways. **Imam al-Ghazali**, for example, considered it a spiritual intuition that anchors all religious experience. In contrast, **Ibn Taymiyyah** emphasized the literal nature of the covenant, reinforcing the idea that no human is born in a state of ignorance about God.

The Ash'ari and Maturidi theological schools—two dominant Sunni approaches—agree on the concept but differ slightly in emphasis. Ash'aris often frame it as a binding proof (hujjah), while Maturidis focus on the human capacity for rational acknowledgment of the divine, enhanced by this pre-temporal agreement.

6. The Covenant in the Hadith Tradition

The Prophetic tradition reinforces the notion of an innate awareness of God. In one narration, the Prophet (pbuh) was asked about those who die in a state of ignorance (ahl al-fatrah). His response, narrated in Musnad Ahmad and considered hasan by some scholars, indicates that such individuals will be tested in the Hereafter. This points to a layered understanding of accountability: the fitrah provides the potential, while revelation activates it.

7. Relevance in Contemporary Context

In an age of increasing secularization, the idea of an inborn belief in God offers a counter-narrative to materialist philosophy. The Islamic worldview insists that belief is not implanted by society but obstructed by it. The rise of atheism, according to this framework, is not a proof against God's existence but a symptom of spiritual amnesia.

The Primordial Covenant remains a critical theological anchor. It challenges Muslims to remember their original testimony and encourages da'wah (inviting others to Islam) not as a call to a new religion, but as a call to remember what the soul already knows.

Chapter 2: Revelation Begins – Aqeedah in the Makkan Period

The emergence of Islam in 7th-century Arabia marked not only a new religious order but a fundamental confrontation with deeply embedded beliefs. The Makkan period, spanning over thirteen years, was a time focused almost entirely on forming the foundation of Aqeedah—the creed of Islam. During this phase, divine revelation did not prioritize legal rulings or societal codes. Instead, it targeted the heart, the conscience, and the metaphysical questions that shaped human purpose.

1. The Landscape of Belief in Pre-Islamic Arabia

Makkan society was not irreligious; rather, it was a culture dominated by **polytheism** (shirk) and a fractured belief system. The Quraysh, the dominant tribe in Makkah, upheld the existence of a supreme deity—**Allah**—but assigned Him partners in divinity. Idols such as **al-Lat**, **al-'Uzza**, and **Manat** represented various forms of intercession. This corrupted monotheism was not atheistic but degraded Tawheed by incorporating pagan elements.

In Surah Az-Zumar (39:3), the Quran records their reasoning:

> *"We only worship them so that they may bring us nearer to Allah in position."*

Thus, the issue was not belief in God's existence, but in corrupting His uniqueness and exclusivity in worship.

2. The First Revelations: A Return to Tawheed

The initial verses revealed to the Prophet Muhammad (pbuh) in the Cave of Hira (Surah Al-'Alaq 96:1–5) introduced no law, no ritual, and no social reform. Instead, they delivered a confrontation with forgetfulness:

"Read in the name of your Lord who created..."

This call was not to recite but to reflect—to return to the innate recognition of the Creator. These verses introduced the Prophet to divine knowledge (Ilm), but their aim was to reawaken the sleeping fitrah of humanity.

Subsequent early revelations, such as Surah Al-Muddathir and Surah Al-Muzzammil, emphasized spiritual discipline, warning of judgment, and calling for personal purification. This spiritual reformation preceded any formal community-building.

3. Core Themes of Makkan Aqeedah

The Makkan surahs consistently revolved around a tight cluster of theological themes:

- **Tawheed (Monotheism):** The affirmation that Allah is One, without partner. Surah Al-Ikhlas served as a concise declaration of this doctrine.

- **Akhirah (Hereafter):** Repeated descriptions of resurrection, accountability, Paradise, and Hell.

- **Risalah (Prophethood):** The authority and truthfulness of the Prophet Muhammad (pbuh), and the continuation of a prophetic tradition.

- **Refutation of Shirk:** Harsh critiques of idol worship, exposing the futility of man-made deities.

- **Moral Accountability:** Belief was framed as a choice with consequences. Surahs like Al-Qiyamah and An-Naba' made belief in the unseen a criterion of salvation.

This emphasis laid the groundwork for a spiritual revolution, one that did not require state power or societal transformation to begin.

4. Opposition to Aqeedah Before Law

The Quraysh did not initially react violently to the personal prayers of Muhammad (pbuh). Their aggression intensified only when he publicly declared the singularity of God and denounced their idols. The threat was not political; it was theological. The rejection of ancestral religion was a disruption of tribal identity and economic stability.

In Surah Sad (38:5), the Quraysh exclaim:

> *"Has he made the gods [only] one God? Indeed, this is a strange thing!"*

Their astonishment reveals the depth of their attachment to multiplicity in worship. The Prophet's message was revolutionary not because of new rituals, but because it invalidated their entire religious worldview.

5. Early Converts and The Internalization of Aqeedah

Figures such as Abu Bakr, Khadijah, Ali ibn Abi Talib, Bilal, and Ammar ibn Yasir accepted Islam not through argument alone but through the moral and metaphysical clarity of its message. For them, belief in one God redefined their sense of justice, dignity, and spiritual purpose.

Bilal's repeated utterance of "Ahad, Ahad" under torture by Umayyah ibn Khalaf was not a political slogan. It was a theological assertion that nothing—not pain, social ostracism, nor death—could dislodge from his heart. The strength of Aqeedah was demonstrated in silence, in resilience, and in the sacrifices of those who found in Tawheed not only truth, but liberation.

6. Revelation as a Method of Purification

Surahs like Al-Shams and Al-Lail revealed the Qur'an's method of moral awakening. Tawheed was presented not merely as a belief but as a light that exposed inner corruption and moral decay. The soul was called to purification (tazkiyah), with success and failure measured by the condition of the heart.

The emphasis on the unseen was deliberate. Belief in what cannot be seen—God, angels, the afterlife—was the measure of sincerity. In Surah Al-Baqarah, believers are described first by their belief in the unseen (يُؤْمِنُونَ بِالْغَيْبِ), showing that Aqeedah begins where physical evidence ends.

7. Theological Structure Without Legal Complexity

During the Makkan period, formal rituals such as obligatory prayer, zakah, fasting, and pilgrimage had not yet been mandated in their full form. Yet the identity of a Muslim was fully formed. It rested on three pillars:

- Belief in the One God
- Belief in the Prophet as His messenger
- Belief in the Hereafter

These three points were enough to draw the line between kufr and iman. No legal code, no constitution, and no judiciary was necessary for Islam to take hold in the soul. Aqeedah, in this phase, was not a set of academic doctrines but a call to wake up to reality.

8. Revelation and the Challenge to False Notions

The Qur'an repeatedly confronted misconceptions about God and the Hereafter. In Surah Al-Ma'arij, the arrogance of man is exposed:

> *"Indeed, man was created anxious: When evil touches him, impatient, and when good touches him, withholding."*

The Qur'an's tone was not always conciliatory. It warned, threatened, and challenged the listener. It described Hellfire in graphic terms, not as punishment for imperfect behavior, but for rejecting the core truths of existence.

This divine rhetoric was designed not to frighten arbitrarily, but to penetrate the hardened hearts of those who denied their own spiritual origins.

Chapter 3: The Core of Aqeedah – The Six Pillars of Faith

Islamic belief is not a vague spirituality or flexible creed. It rests on six clearly defined foundations known as the **Pillars of Iman (Faith)**. These six elements are not optional. They represent the framework through which all theological, spiritual, and ethical commitments are understood. The Prophet Muhammad (pbuh) articulated them clearly in the well-known **Hadith Jibreel**, when the Angel Jibreel asked:

"Inform me about Iman."

The Prophet (pbuh) responded:

> *"To believe in Allah, His angels, His books, His messengers, the Last Day, and to believe in divine decree, the good and the bad of it."*
>
> (Sahih Muslim)

Each of these pillars forms a critical axis of Aqeedah. Together, they provide a worldview that answers the questions of origin, purpose, morality, authority, and destiny.

1. Belief in Allah (Iman Billah)

Belief in Allah begins not with abstract speculation but with a recognition of His absolute uniqueness. The Qur'an asserts:

> *"Say: He is Allah, the One. Allah, the Self-Sufficient. He neither begets nor is born. Nor is there to Him any equivalent."* (Surah Al-Ikhlas 112:1–4)

This belief includes four essential components:

- **Tawheed al-Rububiyyah**: Affirming that Allah alone is the Creator, Sustainer, and Ruler of all things.

- **Tawheed al-Uluhiyyah**: Recognizing that only Allah deserves to be worshipped without any partners.

- **Tawheed al-Asma wa'l-Sifat**: Affirming Allah's names and attributes without distortion, denial, comparison, or asking "how."

Belief in Allah is not merely acknowledging His existence; it is to affirm His rights, submit to His will, and reject all forms of association (shirk), whether hidden or manifest.

2. Belief in the Angels (Iman bil-Mala'ika)

Angels in Islamic belief are not symbolic figures or metaphors. They are real, created from light, devoid of free will, and perpetually obedient to Allah. The Qur'an describes them:

> *"[They] do not disobey Allah in what He commands them but do what they are commanded."* (Surah At-Tahrim 66:6)

Among their known roles:

- **Jibreel (Gabriel)**: Bringer of revelation.

- **Mika'il (Michael)**: Overseer of provision and rain.

- **Israfil**: Assigned to blow the trumpet on the Day of Judgment.

- **Malik**: Guardian of Hell.

- **Munkar and Nakir**: Questioners in the grave.

- **Kiraman Katibeen**: Recording angels.

Belief in angels cultivates an awareness that all deeds are recorded and that one is never alone, even in solitude. It confirms a structured, unseen world functioning with precision and divine order.

3. Belief in the Divine Scriptures (Iman bil-Kutub)

Allah has sent down scriptures to guide humanity across time. These books contain His words, laws, and wisdom, suited to the nations for whom they were revealed. The Qur'an states:

> *"Indeed, We have sent down the Torah, in which was guidance and light... and We gave him the Gospel... and We have revealed to you the Book in truth, confirming what was before it."*
>
> (Surah Al-Ma'idah 5:44–48)

Known revealed books include:

- **The Suhuf of Ibrahim** (now lost)
- **The Tawrah (Torah)** – to Musa (Moses)
- **The Zabur (Psalms)** – to Dawud (David)
- **The Injil (Gospel)** – to Isa (Jesus)
- **The Qur'an** – to Muhammad (pbuh)

While Muslims affirm the divine origin of previous scriptures, belief includes acknowledging their distortion (tahrif) over time. The Qur'an is believed to be the final, preserved revelation, abrogating what came before it.

4. Belief in the Messengers (Iman bil-Rusul)

Messengers are chosen humans sent by Allah to convey His message. They serve as models of moral conduct and as conduits of revelation. The Qur'an names 25 prophets explicitly but indicates that many others were also sent:

> *"And We certainly sent messengers before you. Among them are those whose stories We have told you, and among them are those We have not told you."* (Surah Ghafir 40:78)

Among the most significant:

- **Nuh (Noah)** – the first to be sent to a polytheistic nation.
- **Ibrahim (Abraham)** – known as the father of the prophets.
- **Musa (Moses)** – receiver of the Torah.
- **Isa (Jesus)** – bearer of the Gospel, born miraculously.
- **Muhammad (pbuh)** – the final messenger, sent for all humanity.

Belief in the messengers involves more than respect; it requires affirmation of their truthfulness, obedience to their guidance, and rejection of false claims to prophethood.

5. Belief in the Last Day (Iman bil-Yawm al-Akhir)

The belief in the Hereafter anchors the moral responsibility of the individual. It affirms that life on earth is a test, and that reward and punishment await in an eternal realm. Elements of this belief include:

- **Signs of the Hour**: Including the coming of the Mahdi, return of Isa, Dajjal (Antichrist), Gog and Magog.
- **Death and the Grave**: Where the soul experiences either peace or punishment.

- **Resurrection (Ba'th)**: Reanimation of the body and soul on the Day of Judgment.

- **Judgment (Hisab)**: Weighing of deeds, presentation of records, intercession.

- **Paradise (Jannah)** and **Hellfire (Jahannam)**: Eternal abodes based on faith and deeds.

Surah Al-Zalzalah (99) provides a vivid summary:

> *"So whoever does an atom's weight of good will see it, and whoever does an atom's weight of evil will see it."*

This belief restrains the soul from arrogance and sin, and provides hope in times of injustice or hardship.

6. Belief in Divine Decree (Iman bil-Qadr)

Qadr is the belief that everything that occurs—good or bad—happens by the will, knowledge, and decree of Allah. This includes four essential elements:

- **Knowledge ('Ilm)**: Allah knows all things—past, present, and future.

- **Writing (Kitabah)**: Everything is recorded in **al-Lawh al-Mahfuz**, the Preserved Tablet.

- **Will (Mashiyyah)**: Nothing occurs except by His will.

- **Creation (Khalq)**: Allah is the creator of all things, including actions.

The Qur'an affirms:

> *"Indeed, all things We created with Qadr."* (Surah Al-Qamar 54:49)

This belief harmonizes trust in Allah with the responsibility to act. While humans make choices, those choices unfold within a divine framework that is neither arbitrary nor unjust. It prevents despair in hardship and arrogance in success.

Chapter 4: Aqeedah of the Prophet (pbuh) and the Sahabah

The Aqeedah of Islam was not developed as a theological abstraction in scholarly circles; it was lived and demonstrated in its purest form by the Prophet Muhammad (pbuh) and his noble Companions (Sahabah). Their belief was characterized by clarity, certainty, and submission, free from philosophical entanglements or speculative debate. It emerged through direct revelation and was applied immediately in life, governance, and worship.

1. The Prophet (pbuh) as the First Believer

The Prophet Muhammad (pbuh) embodied perfect belief in Allah. His trust in divine decree, his fear of the Last Day, and his unshakable Tawheed were not theoretical but constant realities that shaped every aspect of his mission. From the earliest moments of revelation, he demonstrated full submission (Islam) and unwavering belief (Iman).

When the command to warn openly was revealed, he stood on Mount Safa and proclaimed the unity of Allah, despite the tribal and political cost. His refusal to compromise on Tawheed—despite wealth, marriage, and leadership being offered in return—showed the depth of his conviction.

The Qur'an described his Aqeedah as one rooted in certainty:

> *"Say: My prayer, my sacrifice, my living and my dying are for Allah, Lord of the worlds. He has no partner. And this I have been commanded..."* (Surah Al-An'am 6:162–163)

His actions matched his words: long hours in prayer, supplication in private, and reliance on Allah in hardship and battle alike.

2. The Method of Teaching Aqeedah

The Prophet (pbuh) did not present theology through abstraction. His instruction was always practical and rooted in the Qur'an. He clarified the six pillars of Iman, warned against shirk, and taught the names and attributes of Allah through prayer and example.

In hadiths such as the one where a slave girl is asked, "Where is Allah?" and she replies, "Above the heavens," the Prophet (pbuh) affirms her belief without philosophical qualification. This shows the clarity and straightforwardness of Aqeedah in his teaching.

He frequently emphasized sincerity (ikhlas), cautioning against ostentation in worship. He warned against exaggeration of the righteous, as seen when he forbade turning graves into places of worship. He maintained strict boundaries between divine rights and human reverence, preserving Tawheed from gradual corruption.

3. The Sahabah: Transmission Without Innovation

The Companions received Aqeedah directly from the Prophet (pbuh). Their understanding was shaped by witnessing revelation, questioning the Messenger, and applying his instructions in real time. Their belief was not derived through dialectic or analogical reasoning; it was rooted in submission to authentic speech.

Abu Bakr As-Siddiq's belief was evident in his constancy during the Prophet's passing, his leadership of the ummah, and his war against the apostates. He firmly upheld that Islam required belief and action, refusing to separate the two.

Umar ibn Al-Khattab's Aqeedah was built on clarity and justice. He implemented the laws of Islam without hesitation, fearing Allah profoundly and often questioning himself. His awareness of accountability in the Hereafter guided every decision.

Uthman ibn Affan's sense of responsibility before Allah led to his deep modesty and generosity. He would cry while hearing verses of the Qur'an and was known to spend the night in voluntary prayer.

Ali ibn Abi Talib's knowledge of Tawheed and his caution against exaggeration in his name show the Sahabah's resistance to sectarianism or veneration of any person beyond measure. When groups tried to claim divine qualities for him, he burned them and declared their belief kufr.

Each Companion, in his own way, preserved the essence of Aqeedah as transmitted by the Prophet (pbuh)—unmixed with superstition, extremism, or theological speculation.

4. Belief in the Unseen (Ghayb) Without Hesitation

The Sahabah believed in matters of the unseen without doubt or resistance. Whether it was the punishment of the grave, the questions of Munkar and Nakir, or the intercession of the Prophet on the Day of Judgment, their hearts accepted these truths without needing metaphysical justifications.

When verses describing Paradise or Hell were recited, they wept. When reminded of Allah's mercy or punishment, their behavior changed. Their belief was not limited to intellectual agreement but was transformative.

During the digging of the trench in the Battle of Khandaq, the Prophet (pbuh) foretold the future conquest of the empires of Persia and Rome. Despite hunger and threat, the Sahabah believed without skepticism.

5. Attitude Toward Bid'ah (Innovation)

The Companions were particularly cautious regarding innovations in belief. They feared misguidance even in seemingly small deviations.

Ibn Mas'ud warned:

> *"Follow and do not innovate, for you have been sufficed."*

They adhered strictly to what the Prophet (pbuh) taught regarding Allah's attributes, the unseen world, and eschatological events. They neither added speculative interpretation (ta'wil) nor negated revealed descriptions of Allah. When Allah described Himself as being above the Throne or as having hands, they affirmed it as befitting His majesty, without likening Him to creation.

6. Unity on Belief Despite Diversity of Backgrounds

The Sahabah included former polytheists, Jews, Christians, and idolaters, yet they all held to a unified Aqeedah. There was no sectarian split during the Prophet's life nor under the rightly guided caliphs in matters of belief.

The unity of Aqeedah was maintained by the clarity of revelation, the trustworthiness of the Prophet's teaching, and the willingness of the Sahabah to submit without introducing foreign ideas.

When disputes occurred, they returned to the Prophet (pbuh) or the Qur'an for clarification. They did not develop theological schools; instead, they preserved the original expressions of faith through loyalty to revelation and companionship with the Messenger.

7. Role of the Sahabah in Preserving and Transmitting Aqeedah

After the Prophet's death, the Sahabah took on the responsibility of preserving the faith. They taught the next generation—known as the Tabi'in—without dilution. Their transmission of the Qur'an, hadith, and understanding of creed ensured that the Aqeedah remained pure in its earliest generation.

Their consensus (ijma') was seen as a safeguard. Imam Ahmad ibn Hanbal later remarked that one of the signs of Ahl al-Sunnah was adherence to the understanding of the Sahabah. Deviations began when later generations attempted to interpret the Qur'an and Sunnah through philosophical frameworks not used by the Prophet (pbuh) or his companions.

Chapter 5: The Early Sects and the Umayyad Period

The death of the Prophet Muhammad (pbuh) marked the beginning of a new phase in the history of Islamic thought. While the foundation of Aqeedah had been firmly laid during the Prophetic era and preserved through the consensus of the Companions, the political and social shifts that followed gave rise to internal divisions. These early deviations did not arise from revelation but from political conflict, philosophical influence, and personal interpretation, leading to the emergence of distinct sects. The Umayyad period (661–750 CE) became a critical epoch for the early development of theological divergence.

1. The Political Roots of Sectarianism

The assassination of Uthman ibn Affan (RA) in 656 CE created a vacuum that exposed underlying tensions. The ensuing civil wars—beginning with the Battle of the Camel and followed by the Battle of Siffin—placed Ali ibn Abi Talib (RA) and Mu'awiyah ibn Abi Sufyan (RA) at the center of political dispute. These events were initially political in nature, but they gave birth to sects that later formulated unique theological positions.

The Khawarij were the first to break away. Emerging after the arbitration between Ali and Mu'awiyah, they declared both sides as apostates for accepting human judgment over divine command. Their rebellion at Nahrawan in 658 CE was crushed militarily, but their ideological legacy endured.

2. The Rise of the Khawarij

The Khawarij (from *kharaja*, "to exit") adopted an uncompromising stance on sin and judgment. They believed that a major sinner (*fasiq*) was no longer a Muslim, rejecting the distinction between sin and disbelief.

Their creed included:

- **Takfir for major sins**: They excommunicated Muslims who committed what they deemed major offenses.

- **Denial of intercession**: They rejected any intercession by the Prophet (pbuh) on behalf of sinful believers.

- **Literalism**: Their readings of the Qur'an ignored contextual interpretation or the explanations given by the Prophet's companions.

Their influence extended across regions through rebellion and radical preaching, contributing to an environment where theological violence accompanied political dissent. Their approach to Aqeedah lacked balance, divorcing divine mercy from divine justice.

3. The Emergence of the Shi'a

In contrast to the Khawarij's rejection of Ali, another faction elevated him beyond normative boundaries. While many Muslims viewed Ali as a rightful caliph and a virtuous Companion, the Shi'a developed distinct theological beliefs around his role and lineage.

Key developments in early Shi'i doctrine during the Umayyad era included:

- **Divine designation (nass)**: The belief that Ali was divinely appointed by the Prophet (pbuh) as his successor.

- **Infallibility ('ismah)**: Claims of sinlessness for the Imams.

- **Occultation (ghaybah)**: The belief that the final Imam went into hiding and would return as a messianic figure.

Though not all Shi'i groups held the same views, this era witnessed the gradual evolution of ideas that diverged from the creed practiced by the Companions. By the late Umayyad period, groups such as the Zaydis, Imamiyyah, and Isma'ilis had begun to crystallize.

4. Qadariyyah and Denial of Divine Decree

Theological debate became more pronounced with the rise of Qadariyyah, a group that emphasized free will to the point of denying Allah's decree over human actions.

Key figures in the emergence of this sect included:

- **Ma'bad al-Juhani** (d. 699 CE): Considered the first to publicly preach Qadari views in Damascus.

- **Ghaylan al-Dimashqi**: A vocal proponent of Qadari ideas under the Umayyads.

The Qadariyyah denied that Allah had foreordained human actions, arguing instead that humans created their own deeds independently. This was in stark contrast to the clear teaching of the Prophet (pbuh), who said:

> *"The first people to debate concerning Qadar were Ma'bad al-Juhani and his companions."*
>
> (Sunan Abi Dawud)

Companions like Ibn Umar (RA) openly rejected the views of the Qadariyyah, considering their doctrine to be misguidance. This confrontation between traditional belief and speculative theology signaled the start of kalam (theological dialectic) as a discipline.

5. The Umayyad Caliphate and the Institutionalization of Creed

The Umayyad dynasty, while often viewed through a political lens, played a complex role in the development of religious doctrine. The caliphs, ruling from Damascus, sought to preserve Islamic orthodoxy in the face of growing sectarian threats.

- **Abdul Malik ibn Marwan (r. 685–705 CE)** centralized religious authority and emphasized the use of Arabic in administration and religious discourse.

- **Al-Walid and Umar ibn Abd al-Aziz** supported scholars and promoted Qur'anic learning and hadith transmission.

Though the Umayyad rulers were not theologians, their support for hadith scholars and jurists helped counteract the spread of deviant creeds. However, political motivations also led to instances of excessive control, such as forced cursing of Ali from pulpits, which caused further sectarian tension and gave ideological ammunition to oppositional groups.

6. The Role of the Tabi'in

The Tabi'in—the generation after the Companions—played a crucial role in preserving authentic Aqeedah during this period. Figures like **Hasan al-Basri**, **Ata ibn Abi Rabah**, and **Saeed ibn al-Musayyib** rejected the innovations of the Qadariyyah and warned against speculative reasoning in matters of creed.

Hasan al-Basri, while known for his eloquence and spirituality, was particularly forceful in condemning the theological deviation of his time. His students inherited this concern, laying the groundwork for later Sunni orthodoxy, particularly in response to the rise of the Mu'tazilah in the Abbasid period.

7. Early Signs of Philosophical Influence

Though full-scale philosophical theology would emerge later under the Abbasids, traces of foreign influence began to appear during the Umayyad era. Translations of Greek, Persian, and Indian texts in centers like Harran and Alexandria slowly introduced foreign ideas into Muslim intellectual life.

These influences would not fully shape Islamic discourse until the translation movement under the Abbasids, but they laid the groundwork for groups like the Mu'tazilah to later blend revelation with rationalist frameworks. The Sahabah and early scholars, however, responded to these developments by reasserting the sufficiency of revelation and the danger of speculative interpretation in the realm of Aqeedah.

Chapter 6: The Abbasid Era and the Rise of Theology (Kalam)

The Abbasid Caliphate (750–1258 CE) ushered in a transformative period for Islamic civilization. With the capital relocated from Damascus to Baghdad, the empire became a melting pot of cultures, philosophies, and intellectual currents. Under Abbasid rule, access to foreign knowledge expanded dramatically, especially through the translation movement, which introduced Greek, Persian, and Indian thought into Arabic. It was within this rich and volatile intellectual environment that **Ilm al-Kalam**—the discipline of speculative theology—took form and gained influence. This new theological activity sought to define and defend Islamic beliefs through rational argumentation, leading to both refinement and controversy in the articulation of Aqeedah.

1. The Translation Movement and the Rise of Rationalism

The House of Wisdom (*Bayt al-Hikmah*) in Baghdad became a central institution for translating works of logic, philosophy, and medicine. Prominent texts by Plato, Aristotle, Plotinus, Galen, and others were rendered into Arabic. Muslim intellectuals began engaging with Hellenistic concepts such as causality, substance, essence, and the nature of the divine.

While this influx of knowledge strengthened the scientific and medical sciences, it also posed challenges to Islamic theology. Greek metaphysics, particularly Aristotelian logic and Neoplatonist cosmology, introduced paradigms that contrasted sharply with the Qur'anic worldview. Questions about divine attributes, the eternity of the world, and the limits of human reason became focal points for debate.

2. The Muʿtazilah: Rationalist Theology Emerges

The Muʿtazilah emerged as the first fully developed theological school in the Abbasid era. Originally influenced by the teachings of Wasil ibn Ata (d. 748 CE), the school reached its intellectual maturity under scholars like Abu al-Hudhayl al-'Allaf and al-Nazzam. Their principles emphasized human free will, rational inquiry, and the justice of Allah.

The Muʿtazilah advanced five core doctrines:

- **Tawheed** – Rejection of anthropomorphism and affirmation of Allah's unity through denial of real attributes.

- **Adl (Divine Justice)** – Belief that humans must have free will for divine justice to be meaningful.

- **Al-Wa'd wa al-Wa'id** – Promise and threat: sinners who die without repentance will face eternal punishment.

- **Manzilah bayna al-Manzilatayn** – The grave sinner is neither a believer nor a disbeliever.

- **Enjoining Right and Forbidding Wrong** – An obligation to promote moral reform, even against rulers.

They used Greek logic and dialectics to articulate their positions, often framing debates through syllogisms and speculative reasoning. Though they positioned themselves as defenders of Islam against atheists and heretics, their methodology diverged sharply from that of the Salaf (early generations).

3. The Mihnah: Inquisition and the State's Role in Theology

During the reign of Caliph al-Ma'mun (r. 813–833 CE), the Muʿtazili doctrine gained official patronage. Influenced by his admiration for Greek philosophy and rationalist theology, al-Ma'mun instituted the **Mihnah**—an inquisition that tested scholars on their belief in the createdness of the Qur'an.

The Mu'tazilah held that the Qur'an was a created entity, not the uncreated speech of Allah. This doctrine, drawn from their commitment to Tawheed and influenced by philosophical atomism, directly conflicted with traditional Sunni belief.

Scholars who refused to affirm the Qur'an as created were imprisoned, tortured, or silenced. Among them was **Imam Ahmad ibn Hanbal**, whose steadfastness during the Mihnah became legendary. Despite imprisonment and physical punishment, he refused to alter his position, maintaining that the Qur'an was the uncreated word of Allah.

The Mihnah continued under caliphs al-Mu'tasim and al-Wathiq, ending with al-Mutawakkil in 847 CE, who reversed the policy and restored Sunni orthodoxy. The episode highlighted the danger of state-imposed theology and underscored the resilience of traditional beliefs under duress.

4. The Ash'ari and Maturidi Responses

As the influence of Kalam spread, responses to rationalist theology began to take shape. **Abu al-Hasan al-Ash'ari** (d. 936 CE), initially a Mu'tazili theologian, broke from his former teachers and began advocating a middle path. While he accepted the use of logic and dialectics, he did so to defend Sunni doctrines, not alter them.

The Ash'ari creed affirmed:

- The reality of Allah's attributes without likening them to creation.
- The uncreated nature of the Qur'an.
- The compatibility of divine omnipotence with human responsibility.

- That Iman includes belief in the heart and affirmation by the tongue, with action as a completion.

Abu Mansur al-Maturidi (d. 944 CE), working independently in Transoxiana, developed a similar approach. He upheld the traditional Sunni creed but employed reasoned argument to protect it from speculative extremes.

Both schools sought to defend orthodox Aqeedah from rationalist overreach while incorporating aspects of dialectical methodology. Their influence became dominant in many parts of the Islamic world, especially among the Shafi'i, Hanafi, and Maliki jurists.

5. Hanbali Traditionalism and the Athari School

In contrast to the theologians of Kalam, Hanbali scholars remained committed to a literalist and narrational approach. They rejected speculative theology entirely, insisting that matters of Aqeedah must be derived solely from the Qur'an and authentic Sunnah, as understood by the Companions.

The **Athari** creed:

- Affirmed Allah's names and attributes without *ta'wil* (figurative interpretation), *tashbih* (comparison), or *ta'til* (negation).

- Rejected the use of kalam and Greek logic in religious matters.

- Maintained that Iman consists of belief in the heart, affirmation by the tongue, and action by the limbs, and that it increases and decreases.

Figures like **Ibn Battah**, **Abu Ya'la**, and later **Ibn Taymiyyah** developed this framework, defending it against both Mu'tazili and

Ash'ari criticisms. For the Athari scholars, reliance on revelation was not only sufficient but also necessary to preserve the purity of belief.

6. Theological Diversity in the Abbasid Courts and Madaris

Under later Abbasid caliphs, particularly during the tenth and eleventh centuries, intellectual life flourished in the form of **madrasahs** and scholarly institutions. The **Nizamiyyah** schools, founded by Nizam al-Mulk in the 11th century, prominently featured Ash'ari scholars such as **Imam al-Ghazali**, who integrated Sufism, philosophy, and theology in a cohesive Sunni framework.

Disagreements persisted between the Hanbali traditionalists and the rationalist theologians, but within the Sunni fold, a broad tolerance emerged, provided that core beliefs—Tawheed, Prophethood, and eschatology—remained intact.

This era produced a wealth of theological literature, including:

- *Al-Ibanah* by al-Ash'ari.
- *Al-Tamhid* by Abu Shakur al-Salimi (Maturidi).
- *Usul al-Sunnah* by Ahmad ibn Hanbal.
- *Ihya' Ulum al-Din* by al-Ghazali, which fused spiritual purification with theological doctrine.

Chapter 7: Ahl al-Sunnah wal-Jama'ah: The Sunni Orthodoxy

The consolidation of Islamic belief and practice during the formative centuries of Islam produced a broad but coherent framework of orthodoxy known as **Ahl al-Sunnah wal-Jama'ah**—literally, "the people of the Sunnah and the community." This term came to represent those Muslims who adhered to the prophetic tradition (*Sunnah*) and the unified body of the Muslim ummah (*Jama'ah*), particularly in matters of creed. It became both a spiritual and theological identifier, distinguishing those who preserved the beliefs of the Prophet (pbuh) and his Companions from emerging theological innovations.

1. Historical Roots of the Term

The term **Ahl al-Sunnah wal-Jama'ah** was first used during the first century of Islam to denote the group that remained upon the consensus of the Companions. It contrasted with the rebellious and divisive groups such as the **Khawarij**, **Shi'a**, and later the **Qadariyyah** and **Mu'tazilah**, who opposed core aspects of mainstream belief.

Scholars like **Abdullah ibn al-Mubarak** (d. 797 CE), **Ahmad ibn Hanbal** (d. 855 CE), and **al-Barbahari** (d. 940 CE) employed the term as a badge of orthodoxy, reinforcing fidelity to revelation and the consensus (*ijma'*) of the early generations.

2. Core Doctrinal Foundations

The belief system of Ahl al-Sunnah wal-Jama'ah is based upon unambiguous sources: the **Qur'an**, the **authentic Sunnah**, and the **ijma'** of the Sahabah and Tabi'in. Its defining features include:

- **Affirmation of all of Allah's Names and Attributes** as revealed, without **ta'wil** (figurative reinterpretation), **tashbih** (comparison), or **ta'til** (denial).

- **Belief in the Uncreatedness of the Qur'an**, as it is the speech of Allah, not a created entity.

- **Recognition of Divine Qadar** (Decree), both the good and the bad, while affirming human moral accountability.

- **Acceptance of the Companions' Virtues**, refraining from cursing or reviling any among them.

- **Rejection of innovative theological claims**, particularly those influenced by speculative reasoning divorced from revelation.

The creed of Ahl al-Sunnah stands balanced between the extremes: between determinism and total free will, between anthropomorphism and denial of divine attributes, and between blind literalism and excessive rationalism.

3. Methodological Unity Amid Diversity

While the unity of belief among Ahl al-Sunnah wal-Jama'ah is grounded in revelation and early consensus, it allows for methodological diversity in theological articulation. This unity encompasses:

- **The Athari School**: Rooted in the Hanbali tradition, led by Ahmad ibn Hanbal, it emphasizes a strictly textualist approach to Aqeedah, avoiding speculative theology altogether.

- **The Ash'ari School**: Founded by Abu al-Hasan al-Ash'ari, it uses rational tools to defend traditional beliefs, especially against the Mu'tazilah.

- **The Maturidi School**: Developed by Abu Mansur al-Maturidi, it shares much with the Ash'ari school but arose independently within the Hanafi context, particularly in Central Asia.

Despite their methodological distinctions, all three schools affirm the essentials of Tawheed, prophethood, the afterlife, the attributes of Allah, and the validity of ijma'. Their coexistence within Sunni orthodoxy reflects a robust intellectual tradition committed to preservation rather than innovation.

4. Relationship with the Four Sunni Madhhabs

The four Sunni legal schools—**Hanafi**, **Maliki**, **Shafi'i**, and **Hanbali**—played a pivotal role in reinforcing the creed of Ahl al-Sunnah. While their primary domain was jurisprudence (*fiqh*), each school aligned itself with Sunni theological norms and often hosted both rationalist and traditionalist scholars.

- **Hanafis** in the eastern provinces often followed Maturidi theology.
- **Malikis** were historically closer to Athari positions, especially in North Africa.
- **Shafi'is** embraced Ash'ari theology through major figures like **al-Juwayni** and **al-Ghazali**.
- **Hanbalis** maintained a strict Athari creed, emphasizing the danger of kalam.

The relationship between fiqh and Aqeedah remained interwoven but compartmentalized, allowing scholars to maintain loyalty to Sunni creed while exploring legal and philosophical complexities within their madhhabs.

5. Defining Deviance and Innovation (Bid'ah) in Creed

The scholars of Ahl al-Sunnah developed rigorous criteria to distinguish between orthodoxy and deviation. Innovations in belief were seen as more dangerous than innovations in practice because they corrupted the core understanding of the religion.

- **Bid'ah in Aqeedah** was classified as major or minor.

- **Major innovations** include denying divine attributes, rejecting the Qur'an's eternal nature, or cursing the Companions.

- **Minor innovations** involve speculative excesses that do not amount to outright heresy but still depart from prophetic teachings.

Key figures like **Ibn Taymiyyah**, **al-Ghazali**, and **al-Shahrastani** discussed the principles of deviation and categorized sects based on their alignment or divergence from foundational Islamic beliefs.

6. Preserving the Creed Through Writings

Ahl al-Sunnah preserved their creed through concise doctrinal treatises, many of which are still studied today. These texts outlined core beliefs in clear language, free of speculative jargon.

Notable creedal works include:

- *Usul al-Sunnah* by Imam Ahmad ibn Hanbal

- *Al-Fiqh al-Akbar* attributed to Imam Abu Hanifah

- *Al-Ibanah* by Abu al-Hasan al-Ash'ari

- *Aqeedah al-Tahawiyyah* by Imam al-Tahawi

- *Luma' al-I'tiqad* by Ibn Qudamah

- *Sharh al-'Aqeedah al-Wasitiyyah* by Ibn Taymiyyah

These texts emphasized clarity, rootedness in revelation, and respect for the understanding of the Salaf. They were not merely theological exercises but practical guides to faith in a world increasingly confronted with heterodox ideologies.

7. Communal Identity and Unity

Ahl al-Sunnah wal-Jama'ah served as a spiritual and social anchor, promoting communal unity in a time of fragmentation. Its emphasis on **ijma'**, the preservation of the Qur'an and Sunnah, and the veneration of the rightly-guided caliphs offered a stable platform for the ummah.

The concept of **al-Jama'ah** was not only about collective belief but also about political unity. The classical Sunni stance discouraged rebellion against Muslim rulers, provided they upheld the essentials of Islam, as civil strife was seen as more harmful than imperfect governance. This balance between theological clarity and political restraint allowed Ahl al-Sunnah to maintain a central place in Islamic civilization, resisting the centrifugal pull of sectarianism and philosophical deviation.

Chapter 8: Belief in Allah's Names and Attributes

Understanding **Allah's Names and Attributes** (*Asma' wa Sifat*) is central to Islamic Aqeedah. It forms the foundation for how Muslims conceptualize the Divine Essence and relate to the Creator. The Qur'an frequently mentions Allah's Names and Attributes, emphasizing their significance for faith and worship. The proper belief regarding these is a critical subject within the theology of Ahl al-Sunnah wal-Jama'ah, as any misinterpretation risks either anthropomorphism or negation of divine reality.

1. The Qur'anic Framework of Divine Names and Attributes

The Qur'an reveals over ninety Names of Allah, many of which correspond to specific Attributes. These Names include those that describe Allah's Essence, such as **Al-Hayy (The Ever-Living)** and **Al-Qayyum (The Sustainer)**, as well as Names that describe His Actions, such as **Al-Khaliq (The Creator)** and **Ar-Rahman (The Merciful)**.

Attributes mentioned in the Qur'an can be broadly classified as:

- **Attributes of Essence (*Sifat Dhatiyyah*)**: eternal qualities intrinsic to Allah's Being, such as **Al-Qadim** (The Eternal) and **Al-Baqi** (The Everlasting).

- **Attributes of Action (*Sifat Filiyyah*)**: qualities related to Allah's interaction with creation, such as **Al-Khaliq** (Creator) and **Al-Muhaymin** (Guardian).

- **Attributes of Perfection**: qualities like **Al-'Alim** (All-Knowing), **Al-Qadir** (All-Powerful), and **Al-Hakim** (The Wise).

The Qur'anic portrayal emphasizes both the transcendence and the immanence of Allah, portraying Him as wholly other than creation but also intimately involved in the cosmos.

2. Theological Challenges: Affirmation without Anthropomorphism

The key theological challenge is to affirm all the divine Names and Attributes as revealed without equating them to the attributes of created beings or distorting their meanings. Islamic theology categorically rejects:

- **Tashbih (Anthropomorphism)**: likening Allah's Attributes to human or created characteristics.

- **Ta'til (Negation)**: denying or nullifying the Attributes entirely.

The principle that safeguards against these extremes is known as **Bila Kayf**—affirmation "without asking how." This approach accepts the literal wording of the Qur'an and Sunnah concerning the Names and Attributes but refrains from delving into speculative explanations or allegorical reinterpretations.

3. The Salaf's Approach to Divine Attributes

The earliest Muslims—the **Salaf al-Salih** (pious predecessors)—held a strict textualist position regarding Allah's Attributes. They accepted the Names and Attributes as they appear in the Qur'an and authentic Sunnah without likening them to creation or denying their reality.

For example:

- The Attribute of **Yad (Hand)** mentioned in the Qur'an is affirmed as true, but its exact nature is unknown and not comparable to human hands.

- The Attribute of **Istiwa' (establishing or rising over the Throne)** is accepted without interpretation or metaphor.

This method was aimed at preserving the transcendence and uniqueness of Allah while maintaining the integrity of revelation.

4. Ash'ari and Maturidi Interpretations

The Ash'ari and Maturidi schools developed nuanced positions to articulate and defend the belief in divine Attributes, especially in response to Mu'tazilite rationalism.

- **Ash'aris** accept the Attributes literally but interpret some metaphorically to avoid anthropomorphism. For example, **Yad** may be interpreted as divine power or authority rather than a physical hand.

- **Maturidis** generally emphasize the literal affirmation of Attributes but allow for figurative interpretations where the literal meaning would imply similarity to creation.

Both schools maintain the principle that Allah's Attributes are eternal, unlike the transient attributes of creatures, and that they do not imply composition or multiplicity in the Divine Essence.

5. The Athari (Traditionalist) Position

The Athari or Hanbali school strictly follows the Salaf's stance: affirm the Attributes as they appear in the texts without figurative interpretation or metaphorical explanation. For them, the divine **Sifat** are beyond human comprehension and must be accepted **bilā kayf**—without delving into "how" or "why." They argue that resorting to allegorical interpretation risks opening the door to doubt and distortion of the text, potentially leading to *ta'til* or *tashbih*.

6. Key Divine Attributes Explored

Several Attributes are frequently emphasized due to their theological importance:

- **Al-Rahman and Al-Rahim (The Most Merciful and The Most Compassionate):** these Names highlight Allah's mercy as the most dominant attribute. Mercy encompasses all His actions and is foundational to human hope.

- **Al-'Adl (The Just):** Allah's justice ensures that all deeds are accounted for and rewarded or punished fairly.

- **Al-Qadir (The All-Powerful):** signifies Allah's unlimited ability to create, sustain, and govern the universe.

- **Al-'Ilm (The All-Knowing):** denotes Allah's perfect knowledge of the past, present, and future, encompassing all seen and unseen realities.

- **Al-Hayy (The Ever-Living):** Allah's life is absolute and necessary, unlike the contingent life of creation.

- **Al-Samad (The Eternal Refuge):** Allah is self-sufficient and independent, the one to whom all creation turns in need.

Each of these Names carries profound implications for worship, reliance, and the believer's relationship with Allah.

7. Implications for Worship and Devotion

The belief in Allah's Names and Attributes shapes the believer's spiritual experience. Recognizing Allah's Mercy inspires hope and repentance; acknowledging His Justice instills accountability and fear of wrongdoing. Trust in His Knowledge and Power strengthens reliance and patience amid trials.

Invoking Allah by His Names is a practice encouraged in the Qur'an and Sunnah, as in the well-known *Asma' al-Husna* (The Most Beautiful Names). These Names become a source of meditation, supplication, and ethical orientation, deeply integrated into Islamic spirituality.

8. Rejection of Philosophical Reductionism

During the Abbasid and later periods, some philosophers and theologians attempted to reduce Allah's Attributes to abstract concepts or deny their independent reality to preserve strict unity.

Ahl al-Sunnah rejected such reductionism, affirming that:

- The Names and Attributes are neither separate entities nor mere human constructs.

- They are real qualities of Allah, inseparable from His Essence, but not divisible parts.

- Denying or distorting any revealed Attribute is tantamount to undermining the Qur'anic message.

This stance preserves both the **transcendence** and **immanence** of Allah in the classical Sunni understanding.

9. Contemporary Reflections

Today, the discussion of Allah's Names and Attributes continues in both traditional and academic Islamic circles. Traditional scholars emphasize returning to the **Salafi methodology** of textual affirmation and avoidance of speculative theology.

Contemporary scholars also address misunderstandings and misrepresentations common in modern contexts, reaffirming the importance of the classical balance: belief grounded in revelation, free from anthropomorphism and philosophical excess.

Chapter 9: Qadr (Divine Decree) and Human Free Will

The intricate balance between **Qadr**—Allah's divine decree—and **human free will** occupies a pivotal place in Islamic theology. This topic addresses fundamental questions about predestination, human responsibility, divine justice, and the nature of God's control over creation. Throughout Islamic history, scholars have sought to articulate a coherent understanding that affirms Allah's absolute sovereignty while preserving meaningful human accountability.

1. Defining Qadr: The Concept of Divine Decree

Qadr literally means "measure," "decree," or "predestination." In Islamic theology, it refers to Allah's complete knowledge, will, and control over all that occurs. Allah's decree encompasses all events, from the grand cosmic scale to the minutiae of daily life.

The Qur'an emphasizes that nothing happens except by Allah's leave:

> *"Indeed, all things We created with predestination." (Qur'an 54:49)*

> *"Say, 'Never will we be struck except by what Allah has decreed for us; He is our protector.'"* (Qur'an 9:51)

This establishes the foundational belief that all existence unfolds according to Allah's prior knowledge and divine will.

2. Components of Qadr

Scholars traditionally divide Qadr into four interrelated components:

- **Knowledge (*Ilm*):** Allah's perfect and eternal knowledge of everything that has happened, is happening, and will happen.

- **Writing (*Kitabah*):** Allah has recorded all that will occur in the Preserved Tablet (*al-Lawh al-Mahfuz*).

- **Will (*Mashi'ah*):** Allah's will is absolute; whatever He wills necessarily occurs.

- **Creation (*Khalq*):** Allah is the Creator of all actions and events, including human deeds.

These components affirm that divine decree is comprehensive and that nothing can occur outside of Allah's design.

3. Human Free Will in Islam

Alongside divine decree, Islam firmly upholds **human free will** (*ikhtiyar*). Humans possess the capacity to choose, intend, and act, and are responsible for these choices.

The Qur'an repeatedly holds people accountable:

> *"Whoever does righteousness—it is for his own soul; and whoever does evil—it is against it."* (Qur'an 45:15)

This accountability presupposes that humans can make genuine choices, not mere automatons compelled by fate.

4. The Theological Tension

The tension arises in reconciling Allah's absolute control and knowledge with human freedom and moral responsibility. If Allah predetermines everything, how can humans be held accountable for their actions?

Different theological schools responded in various ways:

- **The Mu'tazilah:** Emphasized human free will, denying that Allah creates human actions to preserve divine justice. They posited that humans are the true creators of their deeds.

- **The Jabriyah:** Advocated a determinist position, asserting humans have no free will; all actions are compelled by divine decree.

- **Ahl al-Sunnah wal-Jama'ah:** Adopted a middle path, affirming divine decree without negating human choice and responsibility.

5. The Sunni Middle Path: Kasb (Acquisition)

The concept of **Kasb** (acquisition), articulated notably by Imam Ahmad ibn Hanbal and later scholars like al-Ash'ari, presents a nuanced solution:

- Allah **creates** all actions, but humans **acquire** them through intention and choice.

- This means Allah is the ultimate Creator of every act, but human beings are responsible for their acquisition of these acts.

- Human responsibility stems from their intention and choice, even though the power to act is from Allah.

This doctrine preserves divine omnipotence while upholding human accountability.

6. Divine Justice and Wisdom

Belief in Qadr is intertwined with the affirmation of Allah's justice. Since Allah is Al-'Adl (The Just), it would be unjust to punish or reward humans unfairly.

Hence:

- Humans are judged based on their intentions and choices.
- Allah's knowledge and decree do not coerce humans into sin.
- Divine wisdom ensures that decree encompasses human freedom in a manner beyond human comprehension.

This understanding fosters both hope and fear in believers, encouraging righteous deeds and reliance on divine mercy.

7. Implications for Faith and Action

The belief in divine decree and human free will has profound implications:

- **Trust in Allah's Plan:** Believers find solace knowing that everything occurs according to divine wisdom.
- **Active Responsibility:** Humans remain morally accountable and obligated to strive for good.
- **Avoidance of Fatalism:** True faith rejects passivity, emphasizing effort alongside reliance on Allah.
- **Spiritual Patience:** Trials and setbacks are understood as part of divine decree, cultivating patience and perseverance.

This balanced worldview encourages a dynamic engagement with life under the sovereignty of Allah.

8. Reflections in Classical and Contemporary Scholarship

Classical scholars like **Ibn Taymiyyah** emphasized the compatibility of Qadr with free will, insisting that divine decree does not negate human action but rather underpins it. Modern scholars continue to explore this topic, often emphasizing the limits of human understanding regarding divine omniscience and causality. They stress that while the precise mechanics are a matter of divine knowledge, Muslims must affirm both divine decree and personal responsibility.

Chapter 10: Signs of the Hour and Belief in the Unseen

In Islamic Aqeedah, belief in the **Unseen** (*Ghayb*) encompasses accepting realities beyond human perception, including angels, the soul, Paradise and Hell, and crucially, the **Day of Judgment** (*Yawm al-Qiyamah*). Among the most significant elements of this unseen realm are the **Signs of the Hour**—events foretelling the approach of the Last Day. These signs serve both as reminders and as warnings, reinforcing faith in divine justice and the transient nature of worldly life.

1. The Nature of the Unseen in Islam

The **Unseen** refers to all that exists beyond human sensory experience and rational deduction but is known through divine revelation. The Qur'an commands belief in the Unseen as a hallmark of true faith:

> *"Who believe in the Unseen, establish prayer, and spend out of what We have provided for them."* (Qur'an 2:3)

Belief in the Unseen is not optional but a fundamental pillar of Iman (faith), grounding the Muslim's worldview in realities beyond empirical evidence.

2. The Day of Judgment: Core of the Unseen

The **Day of Judgment** is the ultimate event in Islamic eschatology. It is when all human beings will be resurrected and held accountable for their deeds. The Qur'an repeatedly emphasizes this day as:

- The moment of ultimate justice and recompense.
- The occasion when hidden truths are revealed.

- The time when Paradise (*Jannah*) and Hellfire (*Jahannam*) become manifest.

Belief in the Day of Judgment underpins the moral responsibility of humans and motivates ethical behavior.

3. Signs of the Hour: Overview

The **Signs of the Hour** are prophetic indicators that signal the approach of the Last Day. They are divided into:

- **Minor signs:** Events that gradually unfold over time, often social, moral, or natural phenomena.

- **Major signs:** Extraordinary, supernatural occurrences that directly precede the Hour.

These signs are documented extensively in the Hadith literature, especially in collections like Sahih al-Bukhari and Sahih Muslim.

4. Minor Signs of the Hour

Minor signs encompass widespread moral decay, social upheaval, and natural anomalies. Examples include:

- The spread of **ignorance** and abandonment of religious knowledge.

- Increase in **adultery**, **alcohol consumption**, and **dishonesty**.

- Widespread **wealth** but growing **inequality** and **materialism**.

- The prevalence of **false prophets** and the **loss of trustworthiness**.

- Construction of tall buildings as a sign of worldly pride.

These signs are gradual and observable, serving as ongoing reminders to the believer to remain vigilant and righteous.

5. Major Signs of the Hour

The Major signs are dramatic and unmistakable events, occurring close to the Hour:

- **The appearance of the Mahdi:** a just leader who will restore righteousness.

- **The descent of Prophet 'Isa (Jesus) (pbuh):** who will defeat the false messiah (*Dajjal*) and establish justice.

- **The emergence of the Dajjal (Antichrist):** a deceiving figure who will test the faith of people.

- The **Gog and Magog (Ya'juj and Ma'juj):** destructive tribes that will break free and cause widespread chaos.

- Natural upheavals such as the **sun rising from the west**, the **beast of the earth (Dabbat al-ard)**, and massive earthquakes.

These signs confirm the imminence of the Last Day and demand serious attention and preparation.

6. Theological Significance of Belief in the Unseen and Signs

Belief in the Unseen affirms trust in Allah's wisdom and justice beyond human limitations. It is an acknowledgment that divine knowledge transcends human perception.

- The Signs of the Hour warn against complacency and disbelief.

- They reaffirm the temporal nature of this world and the permanence of the hereafter.

- Believers are urged to cultivate patience (*sabr*), sincerity (*ikhlas*), and steadfastness.

This belief enhances the spiritual dimension of Muslim life, connecting the seen world with the unseen realities.

7. Rejecting Speculation and Excess

Islamic orthodoxy cautions against speculative interpretations or exaggerated focus on signs that might distract from core obligations. The Prophet (pbuh) advised:

> *"There is no one who sees a sign of the Hour but that it will not occur until the rest of the signs have occurred."* (Hadith)

This teaches caution against trying to predict the exact timing of the Hour and encourages continuous readiness instead.

8. Impact on Muslim Practice and Ethics

The awareness of the Unseen and the Signs of the Hour shapes ethical conduct:

- It strengthens **moral accountability**, knowing all actions will be judged.

- It encourages **remembrance of death** and the hereafter.

- It inspires **social justice**, aligning with the eventual establishment of divine justice on the Last Day.

- It fosters **humility** before divine power and wisdom.

Muslims integrate these beliefs into daily worship and life decisions, grounding hope and fear within the framework of divine promise.

9. Modern Reflections and Relevance

Contemporary Muslim scholars continue to emphasize the importance of belief in the Unseen, cautioning against dismissing eschatological teachings as mere superstition. They stress that while scientific advancements explain many worldly phenomena, they do not negate the spiritual truths of the Unseen. The Signs of the Hour remain relevant as ethical and spiritual benchmarks rather than literal countdowns, calling the community toward reform and repentance.

Chapter 11: The Legal Foundation in the Life of the Prophet (pbuh)

The life of the Prophet Muhammad (pbuh) represents the cornerstone of Islamic law (*Fiqh*) and jurisprudence (*Usul al-Fiqh*). His personal conduct, legislative decisions, and method of resolving disputes established the legal framework for the Muslim community, shaping the practical implementation of Islamic principles. Understanding this foundation illuminates how divine guidance was manifested in real-life contexts and provides a model for subsequent generations.

1. Revelation as the Source of Legal Guidance

The primary source of Islamic law during the Prophet's life was the **Qur'an**, revealed gradually over 23 years. The Qur'an provided direct commandments, prohibitions, and general principles governing all aspects of life, including worship, social relations, commerce, and criminal justice. This divine text was supplemented and clarified through the Prophet's actions and sayings, ensuring that law was grounded in the revealed will of Allah.

2. The Sunnah: The Living Example

The **Sunnah**—the Prophet's sayings, actions, and tacit approvals—served as a vital complement to the Qur'an. The Prophet (pbuh) did not merely transmit legislation; he embodied it. His personal behavior, decisions in disputes, and leadership style set precedents that guided the community. The Sunnah provided detailed applications of Qur'anic injunctions and addressed issues not explicitly covered in the Qur'an.

3. Legal Reasoning and Flexibility

Despite the divine origin of Islamic law, the Prophet's methodology demonstrated adaptability. He exercised **Ijtihad** (independent reasoning) when direct revelation did not specify a ruling. For example, the Prophet would consider public welfare, justice, and custom when issuing decisions, thereby establishing principles that later jurists expanded upon. His responsiveness to social realities ensured that Islamic law was relevant and practical.

4. The Role of Consensus and Consultation

The Prophet (pbuh) often consulted his companions (*Sahabah*), valuing their input and collective wisdom. This practice foreshadowed the importance of **Shura** (consultation) in Islamic governance and legal processes. While ultimate authority rested with the Prophet as the Messenger of Allah, his engagement with the community created a participatory atmosphere that strengthened legitimacy and compliance.

5. Key Legal Developments During the Prophetic Period

Several legal institutions and principles crystallized during the Prophet's life:

- **Contracts and Transactions:** Regulations on trade, usury (riba), and business ethics were established to ensure fairness.

- **Family Law:** Marriage, divorce, inheritance, and guardianship laws were codified with social justice in mind.

- **Criminal Justice:** Penalties for theft, murder, and adultery were outlined with due process and evidentiary requirements.

- **Public Morality:** Guidelines for prayer, fasting, charity, and pilgrimage provided structure for communal worship.

Each domain reflected both divine commands and the Prophet's practical judgment.

6. The Prophet's Role as Judge and Legislator

The Prophet served as both judge and lawgiver, resolving disputes and issuing judgments based on revelation and reason. His judgments emphasized **equity**, **compassion**, and **public interest**. Importantly, he upheld the principle that law must serve justice, not merely punitive measures. This judicial role reinforced the inseparability of faith and law in Islam.

7. Preservation and Transmission of the Legal Model

The companions meticulously observed and preserved the Prophet's legal rulings and practices. Their transmission became the basis for Islamic jurisprudence after the Prophet's passing. The early Muslim community's commitment to maintaining this legal legacy ensured continuity and unity, even as the Muslim world expanded geographically and culturally.

8. The Prophet's Legal Legacy and Its Influence

The Prophet's legal foundation created a dynamic system that balances divine command with human agency. His example continues to guide Muslim jurists, emphasizing:

- Fidelity to revealed texts.
- Contextual understanding.
- Justice and mercy as core objectives.

This legacy supports ongoing efforts to interpret and apply Islamic law in diverse and evolving contexts.

Chapter 12: Fiqh During the Khulafa Rashidun

The period of the **Khulafa Rashidun**—the Rightly Guided Caliphs—spanning approximately three decades after the Prophet Muhammad's (pbuh) passing, represents a critical era in the development of Islamic jurisprudence (*Fiqh*). These four leaders—Abu Bakr, Umar ibn al-Khattab, Uthman ibn Affan, and Ali ibn Abi Talib—were not only political leaders but also guardians and interpreters of the Shariah. Their governance and legal decisions shaped the application of Islamic law in diverse and expanding Muslim societies.

1. Continuity with the Prophetic Model

The Khulafa Rashidun maintained unwavering commitment to the Qur'an and Sunnah as the primary sources of law. They emphasized following the Prophet's guidance meticulously, seeking to uphold justice and unity within the rapidly growing Muslim state. Their rulings often involved direct reference to these sources, with careful consultation of the companions who had firsthand knowledge of the Prophet's teachings.

2. Abu Bakr's Legal Approach

As the first Caliph, **Abu Bakr** prioritized preserving the Muslim community's cohesion during a time of internal dissent, including the **Ridda Wars** against apostasy. His legal decisions underscored the importance of maintaining the unity of Islam over personal or tribal interests. He set precedents on matters such as the collection of zakat (obligatory charity), insisting on its payment as an obligation regardless of tribal allegiances. Abu Bakr's approach was cautious yet firm, relying heavily on the Qur'an and established Prophetic traditions to reinforce authority.

3. Umar ibn al-Khattab's Judicial Reforms

The second Caliph, **Umar ibn al-Khattab**, is renowned for his expansive legal reforms and administrative innovations. He institutionalized public justice by appointing judges (*qadis*) throughout the empire and established a judiciary system. Umar emphasized **Ijtihad**—the use of reasoned judgment—especially in novel circumstances where explicit texts were silent or ambiguous.

Examples of Umar's jurisprudential decisions include:

- Regulating market transactions to prevent fraud and monopolies.

- Instituting welfare policies like the **Bayt al-Mal** (public treasury) for social justice.

- Adjusting legal rulings to accommodate the realities of diverse populations under Islamic rule.

His pragmatic use of **Maslahah** (public interest) and **Urf** (custom) expanded the flexibility of Islamic law.

4. Uthman ibn Affan's Stewardship of the Law

The third Caliph, **Uthman ibn Affan**, is credited with compiling the definitive text of the Qur'an, which standardized the primary legal source. His tenure involved dealing with the increasing complexity of legal cases as the empire grew. Uthman continued the practice of appointing judges and delegating authority to ensure consistent application of Shariah. Though less noted for new jurisprudential innovations compared to Umar, Uthman's role in preserving the Qur'an ensured clarity and uniformity in legal references.

5. Ali ibn Abi Talib's Legal Reasoning

The fourth Caliph, **Ali ibn Abi Talib**, was known for his deep knowledge of Islamic law and his emphasis on justice. Ali's legal approach combined strict adherence to scriptural sources with a profound sense of equity and moral responsibility. He was keenly aware of the socio-political challenges of his time, often addressing issues of governance, tribal conflicts, and personal disputes with wisdom. Ali's sermons and judgments reflect a balanced use of **Qiyas** (analogical reasoning) and **Ijtihad**, laying groundwork for later juristic methodologies.

6. Jurisprudential Principles Emphasized

During this era, several key principles guided the Khulafa Rashidun's legal decisions:

- **Adherence to the Qur'an and Sunnah:** They consistently referred to the foundational texts.

- **Consensus (*Ijma'*):** The agreement of the Prophet's companions served as a strong source of legal authority.

- **Public Welfare (*Maslahah*):** They recognized the importance of protecting communal interests.

- **Flexibility and Adaptability:** Use of reason and analogical reasoning to address new situations.

These principles collectively contributed to the dynamic evolution of Islamic law.

7. Challenges Faced

The Khulafa Rashidun dealt with unprecedented challenges, including:

- Governing a rapidly expanding empire with diverse populations and customs.

- Balancing tribal loyalties with Islamic legal ideals.

- Addressing emerging political dissent without compromising justice.

- Ensuring fair distribution of resources and wealth.

Their responses laid the foundation for legal pluralism within the Shariah framework.

8. Legacy of the Khulafa Rashidun in Fiqh

The legal groundwork established during the Rightly Guided Caliphs provided a model of governance deeply rooted in divine guidance yet responsive to changing circumstances. Their methods influenced the later development of the major Sunni schools of jurisprudence by emphasizing a balanced approach that integrated textual fidelity with reasoned judgment. This era remains a gold standard for Islamic leadership and jurisprudential integrity.

Chapter 13: Compilation and Codification: The Tabi'un and Beyond

Following the era of the **Khulafa Rashidun**, the Muslim community entered a crucial phase marked by the efforts of the **Tabi'un**—the generation succeeding the Prophet's companions—and later scholars who undertook the monumental task of compiling, preserving, and codifying Islamic knowledge. This period laid the foundational structures for the formal sciences of **Fiqh** (Islamic jurisprudence) and **Hadith** (Prophetic traditions), shaping the intellectual and legal trajectory of Islam.

1. The Role of the Tabi'un in Preserving Knowledge

The **Tabi'un** were the students and followers of the Sahabah (companions). They inherited a rich but still largely oral tradition of the Qur'an, Sunnah, and legal rulings.

Aware of the necessity to preserve these teachings amid rapid expansion and the passage of time, the Tabi'un emphasized:

- Accurate transmission of hadiths and legal opinions.
- Direct learning from the companions.
- Maintaining the integrity of Qur'anic recitation and its application.

Their dedication ensured the continuity and authenticity of Islamic teachings.

2. Early Efforts in Documentation

During the Tabi'un era, oral transmission remained predominant. However, the increasing geographical spread and linguistic diversity necessitated more structured documentation.

Notable among early efforts were:

- Writing down hadiths and legal rulings on various materials like parchment and bones.

- Beginning informal collections of hadith to safeguard against loss or distortion.

- Compiling Qur'anic verses into manuscripts for reference by scholars and judges.

This transitional phase set the stage for systematic codification.

3. The Emergence of Legal Schools and Methodologies

As the Muslim empire grew, regional variations in practice and interpretation appeared. This gave rise to distinct legal methodologies and proto-schools.

Scholars began to:

- Analyze the Qur'an and Sunnah critically.

- Utilize **Qiyas** (analogical reasoning) to derive rulings for new issues.

- Employ **Ijma'** (consensus) as a principle to unify legal opinions.

These intellectual tools were refined by the Tabi'un and their successors to establish coherent legal frameworks.

4. Compilation of Hadith: Foundations of Authenticity

The science of **Hadith Criticism** developed to distinguish authentic Prophetic traditions from weak or fabricated ones.

Key figures such as:

- **Imam Malik ibn Anas**, who compiled the **Muwatta**, a seminal hadith and jurisprudence collection.

- **Al-Zuhri**, an early hadith scholar who pioneered systematic collection and verification.

Their work formalized methodologies based on the chain of narration (*isnad*) and text (*matn*) scrutiny, ensuring the reliability of sources used in legal rulings.

5. The Codification of Legal Principles

The early codification efforts included:

- Defining principles of **Ijtihad** (independent reasoning).

- Establishing criteria for **Ijma'** (consensus) among scholars.

- Systematizing the categories of rulings (obligatory, recommended, permissible, disliked, forbidden).

These codifications clarified the processes by which new legal issues could be addressed within an Islamic framework.

6. The Role of Centers of Learning

Emerging Islamic cities such as **Kufa**, **Medina**, **Damascus**, and **Basra** became hubs of legal scholarship.

Scholars in these cities:

- Specialized in different jurisprudential approaches.

- Taught students who would become influential jurists.

- Engaged in intellectual debates that refined Fiqh.

These centers fostered diversity yet cohesion in Islamic legal thought.

7. Influence of Political and Social Contexts

The codification process was influenced by the political realities of expanding empires:

- The need to govern diverse populations with varying customs prompted jurists to incorporate **Urf** (local custom) where compatible with Shariah.

- The establishment of formal courts required standardized legal procedures.

- State patronage sometimes affected the preservation and propagation of particular legal opinions.

Thus, jurisprudence became both a religious and practical governance tool.

8. Transition to the Classical Period of Fiqh

By the late Tabi'un and early following generations, the foundation for the classical Islamic legal tradition was firmly established.

This period saw:

- The crystallization of the four main Sunni madhhabs (legal schools).

- The production of foundational texts.

- The systematization of Usul al-Fiqh (principles of jurisprudence).

The efforts of the Tabi'un and subsequent scholars ensured the survival and flourishing of Islamic law in a comprehensive and adaptable form.

Chapter 14: The Four Sunni Madhahib: Foundations and Methodologies

The development of Islamic jurisprudence (*Fiqh*) reached a significant milestone with the establishment of the four major Sunni **Madhahib** (legal schools) during the classical Islamic period. These schools—Hanafi, Maliki, Shafi'i, and Hanbali—emerged from the scholarly efforts of jurists who systematized and interpreted the sources of Islamic law within varied cultural and social contexts. Their diverse methodologies provided Muslims with flexible frameworks for applying Shariah across different regions and times.

1. Historical Context of Madhhab Formation

By the 8th and 9th centuries CE, the Muslim world had expanded vastly, encountering numerous cultures, customs, and legal questions previously unaddressed explicitly in the Qur'an and Sunnah. Scholars sought to:

- Preserve unity by anchoring rulings in the Prophet's teachings.
- Address novel issues through reasoned interpretation.
- Maintain coherence in legal application despite regional differences.

This environment catalyzed the crystallization of distinct but complementary legal traditions.

2. Imam Abu Hanifa (699–767 CE) and the Hanafi School

Abu Hanifa is recognized as the founder of the Hanafi madhhab, which became the most widespread school, particularly across South Asia, Turkey, and parts of the Middle East.

Methodological Features:

- Emphasis on **Qiyas** (analogical reasoning) to extend rulings beyond explicit texts.

- Use of **Istihsan** (juristic preference) to achieve equitable outcomes when strict analogies conflicted with public interest.

- Reliance on **Ijma'** (consensus) where available but with openness to scholarly discretion.

- Greater flexibility accommodating local customs (*Urf*) when consistent with Islamic principles.

The Hanafi approach reflects a pragmatic balance between textual adherence and contextual adaptation.

3. Imam Malik ibn Anas (711–795 CE) and the Maliki School

Malik ibn Anas, based in Medina, founded the Maliki madhhab, emphasizing the practice (*'Amal*) of the people of Medina as a source of law alongside the Qur'an and Sunnah.

Methodological Features:

- Prioritization of the **'Amal Ahl al-Madina** (practice of the people of Medina) as reflective of the Prophet's community's living tradition.

- Application of **Maslahah** (public welfare) as a guiding principle.

- Rigorous use of hadith authentication, often rejecting weak narrations.

- Careful limitation on analogical reasoning, favoring established practices.

The Maliki school stresses historical continuity and community practice as vital to legal understanding.

4. Imam Muhammad ibn Idris al-Shafi'i (767–820 CE) and the Shafi'i School

Al-Shafi'i is credited with systematizing the principles of Islamic jurisprudence, founding the Shafi'i madhhab, which spread widely in East Africa, Southeast Asia, and parts of the Arabian Peninsula.

Methodological Contributions:

- Formalization of **Usul al-Fiqh** as a science, categorizing sources and methods of deriving rulings.
- Establishing the Qur'an and Sunnah as primary sources, with explicit hierarchies.
- Recognition of **Ijma'** and **Qiyas** as valid secondary tools.
- Skepticism toward reliance on local custom when contradicting textual evidence.

Al-Shafi'i's methodology introduced intellectual rigor and clarity to jurisprudential discourse.

5. Imam Ahmad ibn Hanbal (780–855 CE) and the Hanbali School

Ahmad ibn Hanbal founded the Hanbali madhhab, known for its strict textualism and caution toward speculative reasoning.

Methodological Characteristics:

- Strong emphasis on authentic **hadith** and the explicit texts of the Qur'an and Sunnah.

- Reluctance to employ **Qiyas** except when absolutely necessary.

- Minimal acceptance of juristic preference or reliance on custom.

- Preference for the understanding of the Prophet's companions and early generations.

The Hanbali school is often associated with conservatism and fidelity to the earliest Islamic sources.

6. Commonalities and Differences Among the Madhahib

While each madhhab developed unique methodologies, they share foundational commitments:

- Acceptance of the Qur'an and Sunnah as primary legal sources.

- Recognition of consensus (*Ijma'*) and analogical reasoning (*Qiyas*), though with varying emphasis.

- A commitment to justice, public interest, and preservation of the Shariah's objectives.

Differences arise from diverse historical circumstances, regional customs, and interpretative priorities, contributing to legal plurality within Sunni Islam.

7. Impact on Islamic Law and Practice

The coexistence of the four madhhabs allows Muslims to navigate their religious duties with flexibility while maintaining doctrinal coherence. Jurists and scholars draw upon these traditions to:

- Issue **fatwas** (legal opinions) suitable for varying contexts.

- Resolve conflicts between textual evidence and contemporary realities.

- Adapt legal rulings without compromising core principles.

The madhhabs collectively form a rich legal heritage that continues to guide Muslim communities worldwide.

8. Transmission and Institutionalization

The four madhhabs gained prominence through:

- Teaching in major centers of learning such as Baghdad, Cairo, and Cordoba.

- Establishment of legal curricula in **madrasas** and courts.

- Endorsement by political authorities seeking legal uniformity.

Their institutionalization fostered a culture of scholarship, debate, and respect for jurisprudential diversity.

9. The Madhhabs in the Modern Era

Despite challenges from reformist movements and modern legal systems, the four Sunni madhhabs remain influential. Contemporary scholars engage with madhhab methodologies to address new issues like bioethics, finance, and human rights, often employing principles of **Ijtihad** informed by classical sources. The madhhabs thus continue to evolve, preserving Islamic law's relevance and vitality.

Chapter 15: Ijma' and Qiyas: Consensus and Analogy in Fiqh

In the evolution of Islamic jurisprudence (*Fiqh*), two foundational tools—**Ijma'** (consensus) and **Qiyas** (analogical reasoning)—play pivotal roles in extending the law beyond explicit textual evidence. These mechanisms enable jurists to interpret and apply the Shariah to new situations, preserving its relevance across time and contexts. Understanding their origins, principles, and applications illuminates the dynamic nature of Islamic legal thought.

1. The Concept and Importance of Ijma'

Ijma' refers to the unanimous agreement of qualified Muslim scholars on a legal ruling concerning a particular issue. It holds a special status in Islamic law as a third primary source after the Qur'an and Sunnah. This principle is grounded in Prophetic traditions indicating that the Muslim community would not collectively agree upon error, ensuring that consensus embodies divine guidance.

2. Types and Scope of Ijma'

Ijma' can occur in various forms, including:

- **Explicit Consensus:** Clear agreement by all qualified scholars.

- **Tacit Consensus:** General acceptance or absence of opposition.

- **Consensus of the Sahabah:** Agreement among the Prophet's companions, regarded as especially authoritative.

The scope of Ijma' may cover:

- Legal rulings.

- Interpretative methods.
- Ethical and social norms within Islamic law.

3. Historical Development of Ijma'

During the Prophet's lifetime, consensus was naturally unified under his leadership. After his passing, the Sahabah's agreements set precedents, and subsequent generations aspired to maintain such unity. The Rightly Guided Caliphs often sought collective agreement before implementing significant policies, establishing Ijma' as a tool for communal legitimacy.

4. Methodological Challenges in Defining Ijma'

Identifying the exact moment and participants of consensus presents challenges:

- Who qualifies as a scholar capable of Ijma'?
- Must consensus be global or can it be regional?
- How is unanimity verified historically?

These questions led to differing views among jurists, influencing their acceptance and application of Ijma'.

5. The Role of Ijma' in Legal Authority

Ijma' serves to:

- Confirm the authenticity of legal rulings.
- Provide closure on disputed issues.
- Strengthen communal unity through shared decisions.

It acts as a binding legal precedent, preventing arbitrary innovation (*bid'ah*) in matters of established law.

6. The Concept and Mechanism of Qiyas

Qiyas, or analogical reasoning, involves extending a known ruling from an original case with a clear legal injunction to a new case sharing the same effective cause (*'illah*). It is a rational tool that enables jurists to address unprecedented situations while maintaining fidelity to the Shariah's principles.

7. The Elements of Qiyas

A valid Qiyas requires four components:

- **Asl (Original case):** The situation with an established ruling.
- **Far' (New case):** The contemporary or novel issue lacking explicit ruling.
- **Hukm (Ruling):** The legal judgment attached to the original case.
- **'Illah (Effective cause):** The shared reason or rationale linking both cases.

This structure ensures that analogies are grounded in sound logic and scriptural bases.

8. Historical Emergence of Qiyas

While the Qur'an and Sunnah provide many explicit rulings, they do not cover every possible legal issue. Early jurists recognized the necessity of reasoning to resolve novel questions. The concept of Qiyas was formalized notably by **Imam al-Shafi'i**, who systematized its methodology in his works, elevating it as a critical instrument in jurisprudence.

9. Applications of Qiyas in Jurisprudence

Qiyas has been employed to:

- Extend prohibitions, such as applying the Qur'anic ban on wine to other intoxicants.

- Determine rulings on new financial transactions by analogy to existing contracts.

- Address emerging ethical dilemmas by identifying common causes with known cases.

Its use exemplifies the balance between textual fidelity and practical reasoning.

10. Criticisms and Alternatives to Qiyas

Certain Islamic groups and scholars have critiqued or limited Qiyas:

- Some viewed it as too speculative, preferring strict textualism.

- The Hanbali school, while accepting Qiyas, emphasized cautious application.

- Other juristic approaches introduced complementary tools like **Istihsan** (juristic preference) and **Maslahah** (public interest) alongside or in place of Qiyas.

These debates highlight the diversity within Islamic legal theory.

11. Interrelation of Ijma' and Qiyas

Ijma' and Qiyas often operate in tandem:

- Ijma' may affirm the validity of a Qiyas-based ruling.

- Qiyas can fill gaps when Ijma' has not been established.

- Together, they form a methodological framework for legal evolution.

This synergy underpins the adaptability and resilience of Islamic law.

12. Contemporary Relevance

In the modern era, Ijma' and Qiyas continue to provide mechanisms for addressing new legal and ethical challenges posed by technological advances, globalization, and societal change. Scholars engage in **Ijtihad** (independent reasoning), often invoking these principles to issue informed and relevant rulings.

Chapter 16: Istihsan, Istislah, and Urf: Contextual Tools of Fiqh

Islamic jurisprudence (*Fiqh*) is characterized by its capacity to adapt to diverse circumstances without compromising the fundamental principles of Shariah. Among the tools enabling this flexibility are **Istihsan** (juristic preference), **Istislah** (consideration of public interest), and **Urf** (custom). These concepts allow jurists to incorporate context, societal needs, and local practices in legal reasoning, balancing strict textual adherence with practical realities.

1. Istihsan: Juristic Preference

Istihsan—literally "to consider good" or "to deem preferable"—is a principle that allows a jurist to depart from a strict analogy (*Qiyas*) or general rule when it leads to hardship, injustice, or outcomes contrary to the objectives of Shariah. It serves as a corrective measure, prioritizing equitable solutions over rigid legal formalism.

2. Origins and Development of Istihsan

The concept of Istihsan was notably advanced by **Imam Abu Hanifa**, who employed it to soften legal rulings when strict analogical reasoning produced excessive hardship. His approach reflected a desire to uphold the spirit of the law, emphasizing mercy and public welfare. Later scholars debated its scope and legitimacy, with some criticizing it for potential subjectivity, while others defended it as essential for justice.

3. Applications of Istihsan

Istihsan is typically invoked to:

- Avoid legal rulings that cause undue difficulty.
- Overrule conflicting analogies when a preferable alternative better serves justice.

- Resolve conflicts between textual evidence and public interest.

For example, it might be used to permit a contractual condition that strict analogy would invalidate but is widely accepted as fair.

4. Istislah: Consideration of Public Interest

Istislah refers to juristic reasoning grounded in the pursuit of **Maslahah** (public interest or welfare), even in cases where explicit textual evidence is silent. It serves to preserve essential objectives of Shariah, such as protection of religion, life, intellect, lineage, and property.

5. Foundations and Theoretical Framework of Istislah

The classical formulation of Istislah emerged through scholars like **Al-Ghazali**, who argued that actions promoting general welfare and preventing harm align with the divine will, provided they do not conflict with explicit texts. This principle allows jurists to develop rulings responsive to changing social realities and emergent challenges.

6. Examples of Istislah in Jurisprudence

Istislah underpins many legal rulings designed to:

- Facilitate commercial transactions ensuring market stability.

- Regulate public health measures.

- Address environmental protections.

Its application ensures that Islamic law remains vibrant and relevant.

7. Urf: Custom in Islamic Law

Urf—meaning “custom” or “common practice”—represents the prevailing habits and norms of a community. Islamic jurisprudence recognizes Urf as a legitimate source of law when it does not contradict the Qur'an, Sunnah, or established consensus.

8. Significance of Urf in Legal Rulings

Urf allows jurists to:

- Adapt rulings to cultural contexts.
- Validate local commercial practices.
- Resolve ambiguities by referencing accepted social behaviors.

This principle acknowledges the diversity of Muslim communities while preserving core religious tenets.

9. Conditions for the Acceptance of Urf

For Urf to influence legal rulings, it must be:

- Widely known and practiced.
- Not conflicting with explicit scriptural injunctions.
- Reasonable and not harmful.

These conditions safeguard against arbitrary customs overriding Islamic principles.

10. Interaction Among Istihsan, Istislah, and Urf

Though distinct, these tools often interplay:

- Istihsan may rely on Urf to justify juristic preference.
- Istislah may incorporate prevailing customs to advance public interest.

- Together, they provide a holistic framework for contextualized jurisprudence.

Their combined use reflects the dynamic and pragmatic nature of Fiqh.

11. Historical Debates and Controversies

Throughout Islamic history, scholars debated the permissibility and extent of these tools. Some traditionalists feared overuse could undermine textual authority, while pragmatists emphasized their necessity for justice and adaptability. Such discussions shaped the boundaries and methodologies of Islamic legal reasoning.

12. Contemporary Applications

In the modern world, Istihsan, Istislah, and Urf are vital in:

- Addressing novel financial instruments.
- Regulating technological advancements.
- Reconciling Islamic law with pluralistic societies.

They enable jurists to issue rulings that honor Shariah's principles while meeting contemporary needs.

Chapter 17: Maqasid al-Shariah: Objectives of Islamic Law

Islamic law (*Shariah*) is not merely a collection of legal rulings but a comprehensive system designed to achieve specific higher purposes that benefit individuals and society. These purposes are known as **Maqasid al-Shariah**, or the objectives of Islamic law. Understanding these objectives is essential to grasp the wisdom behind legal injunctions and the dynamic application of Islamic jurisprudence.

1. The Concept of Maqasid al-Shariah

The term **Maqasid** means "goals" or "objectives." In the context of Shariah, it refers to the divine intents behind the legal framework revealed by Allah. The Maqasid serve as a guiding principle for interpreting laws and ensuring that the spirit of Islam is fulfilled alongside the letter of the law.

2. Historical Development

Although implicit in the Qur'an and Sunnah, the formal study of Maqasid al-Shariah emerged prominently with scholars such as **Imam al-Ghazali** (11th century CE), who articulated that Shariah aims to preserve and promote human welfare. Later jurists refined these concepts into a structured hierarchy, influencing legal theory and practice.

3. The Five Essential Objectives (Al-Daruriyyat)

Classical scholars generally agree on five fundamental objectives that Shariah seeks to protect:

- **Protection of Religion (Hifz al-Din):** Safeguarding faith, ensuring freedom to worship, and preserving Islamic identity.

- **Protection of Life (Hifz al-Nafs):** Defending human life against harm, violence, and injustice.

- **Protection of Intellect (Hifz al-'Aql):** Preserving reason and mental capacity by prohibiting substances and behaviors that impair judgment.

- **Protection of Lineage (Hifz al-Nasl):** Maintaining family structure and lineage through regulations on marriage, inheritance, and sexual conduct.

- **Protection of Property (Hifz al-Mal):** Securing ownership rights, prohibiting theft, fraud, and ensuring fair economic transactions.

4. Classification Beyond the Essentials

Beyond these essentials, scholars identified secondary and tertiary objectives, including:

- **Facilitation and Ease:** Laws should not impose unnecessary hardship.

- **Prevention of Harm:** Avoidance of detrimental actions even if not expressly forbidden.

- **Promotion of Good:** Encouragement of virtuous conduct and societal welfare.

This hierarchy ensures a balanced and flexible legal system.

5. Sources Supporting Maqasid al-Shariah

The Qur'an and Sunnah repeatedly emphasize mercy, justice, and benefit, providing textual bases for Maqasid:

- Verses advocating justice (*Adl*) and compassion.

- Prophetic sayings underscoring the preservation of life and intellect.

- Legal principles allowing exceptions in cases of hardship or necessity.

These sources reflect divine wisdom embedded in Shariah.

6. Maqasid and Legal Interpretation

Maqasid provide jurists with criteria to:

- Resolve conflicts between texts.

- Adapt rulings to changing circumstances.

- Prioritize objectives when legal provisions seem at odds.

For example, when strict application of a law causes harm, Maqasid guide scholars toward mitigating measures.

7. Maqasid and Ijtihad

The exercise of **Ijtihad** (independent reasoning) is informed by Maqasid, as scholars seek to fulfill the law's underlying purposes rather than rigid formalism. This approach empowers jurists to issue relevant rulings on contemporary issues while remaining faithful to Islamic principles.

8. Maqasid in Contemporary Legal Thought

Modern Islamic scholars increasingly emphasize Maqasid as a framework for:

- Reforming Islamic law to address human rights.

- Reconciling Shariah with modern governance and international law.

- Encouraging ethical economic models and environmental stewardship.

This evolution demonstrates Maqasid's enduring relevance.

9. Maqasid and Public Interest (Maslahah)

The objectives of Shariah closely intersect with the concept of **Maslahah**, or public interest, emphasizing collective welfare. Legal rulings guided by Maqasid inherently seek to promote societal well-being alongside individual rights.

10. Maqasid and the Prevention of Harm (Mafsadah)

Shariah also aims to prevent **Mafsadah** (harm or corruption), balancing benefits and harms to achieve justice. The principle of avoiding harm informs many legal provisions and underlies Maqasid's application.

11. Flexibility Within Shariah Through Maqasid

Maqasid allow Shariah to respond flexibly to new contexts without compromising core values. By focusing on objectives rather than rigid forms, Islamic law maintains its capacity for dynamic interpretation.

Chapter 18: Fiqh of Ibadat: Acts of Worship

In Islamic jurisprudence, *Ibadat* (acts of worship) form a core category of legal rulings that govern the relationship between the servant and Allah. These acts are characterized by their devotional nature, obedience to divine commands, and specific prescribed forms. The *Fiqh of Ibadat* systematically addresses the rules and regulations pertaining to worship, ensuring that these acts are performed correctly, with sincerity, and in accordance with the Shariah.

1. Definition and Scope of Ibadat

Ibadat literally means "servitude" or "worship." In legal terms, it refers to actions performed to fulfill religious duties ordained by Allah. These include rituals such as prayer (*Salah*), fasting (*Sawm*), almsgiving (*Zakat*), pilgrimage (*Hajj*), and other forms of worship. The *Fiqh of Ibadat* explores the conditions, pillars, and validity of these acts.

2. Distinction Between Ibadat and Mu'amalat

Islamic law broadly divides rulings into *Ibadat* (worship) and *Mu'amalat* (social transactions). While *Ibadat* governs rituals and spiritual obligations, *Mu'amalat* regulates interpersonal dealings such as contracts, sales, and criminal law. This distinction underscores the unique nature of worship acts, which primarily concern the individual's direct obligations to Allah.

3. Sources for Fiqh of Ibadat

The primary sources for *Ibadat* jurisprudence are:

- The **Qur'an**, containing direct commandments for worship.

- The **Sunnah** of the Prophet (pbuh), providing detailed guidance on performance.

- Consensus (*Ijma'*) and analogical reasoning (*Qiyas*) applied to worship matters.

These sources ensure both textual and practical precision in worship.

4. Principles Governing Ibadat

Key principles include:

- **Intent (*Niyyah*):** Essential for all acts of worship; the action must be done solely for Allah.

- **Purity (*Taharah*):** Ritual purity is a prerequisite for validity, including ablutions (*Wudu*) and bath (*Ghusl*).

- **Timeliness:** Many acts, such as prayer and fasting, have designated times.

- **Conditions and Pillars:** Each act of worship has specific conditions and essential components that must be fulfilled.

5. Salah: The Pillar of Worship

Salah (prayer) occupies a central position as the first obligatory act after belief.

It involves specific physical postures, recitations, and timings.

The *Fiqh* of Salah elaborates on:

- The number of daily prayers.

- Conditions of validity such as facing the Qiblah.

- Situations invalidating the prayer.

- Permissible concessions (e.g., combining prayers).

6. Sawm: Fasting and Its Regulations

Fasting during Ramadan is obligatory and regulated by detailed rules:

- Abstention from food, drink, and other invalidators from dawn to sunset.

- Exemptions for the sick, travelers, and certain other categories.

- Make-up fasts and expiations for intentional violations.

- The spiritual dimension emphasizing self-restraint and consciousness of Allah.

7. Zakat: Obligatory Almsgiving

Zakat is a mandatory charity purposed to purify wealth and assist those in need.

Fiqh addresses:

- Conditions for obligation, including minimum wealth (*nisab*).

- Calculation of different categories of wealth.

- Eligible recipients.

- Distinctions between Zakat and voluntary charity (*Sadaqah*).

8. Hajj and 'Umrah: Pilgrimage Rites

The pilgrimage to Makkah, Hajj, is a once-in-a-lifetime obligation for those who meet conditions of capability.

Fiqh specifies:

- The rituals to be performed in specific sequences and times.
- The Ihram state, including restrictions during pilgrimage.
- Differences between obligatory Hajj and the lesser pilgrimage, 'Umrah.
- Penalties and compensations for violations.

9. Other Acts of Worship

Additional acts covered under *Fiqh of Ibadat* include:

- **Dua (Supplication):** Guidelines on etiquette and conditions.
- **Dhikr (Remembrance of Allah):** Recommended practices to maintain spiritual awareness.
- **Jihad (Striving in Allah's cause):** Specific rulings related to defensive and spiritual efforts.
- **Tawaf and Sa'i:** Rituals integral to pilgrimage.

10. Flexibility and Concessions in Ibadat

Islamic law incorporates leniency for hardship in worship acts, such as:

- Allowing tayammum (dry ablution) when water is unavailable.

- Permitting fasting to be postponed due to illness.

- Combining or shortening prayers during travel.

These concessions demonstrate Shariah's mercy and accommodation of human circumstances.

11. Role of Intention and Sincerity

Central to *Ibadat* is *Niyyah*—the intention behind actions. Without sincere intention directed toward Allah, even formally correct acts lose their spiritual validity. This emphasis differentiates ritualistic compliance from genuine worship.

12. Impact of the Fiqh of Ibadat on Muslim Life

The legal framework governing acts of worship shapes not only individual spirituality but also communal identity and societal rhythm. Through adherence to *Fiqh* rulings, Muslims cultivate discipline, consciousness of God, and a sense of belonging to a global faith community.

Chapter 19: Fiqh of Mu'amalat: Social Transactions

The **Fiqh of Mu'amalat** deals with the laws and regulations governing human interactions and transactions within society. Unlike *Ibadat*, which pertains to worship and the individual's relationship with Allah, *Mu'amalat* focuses on the rights and duties between people, ensuring justice, fairness, and harmony in social, economic, and political dealings. This branch of Islamic jurisprudence plays a vital role in structuring communal life and upholding ethical standards.

1. Definition and Scope of Mu'amalat

The Arabic term *Mu'amalat* means "transactions" or "dealings." It encompasses a wide range of activities including contracts, trade, marriage, inheritance, criminal justice, and governance. The objective is to regulate these interactions according to Shariah principles that promote justice, prevent harm, and protect rights.

2. Sources of Mu'amalat Law

Like all Islamic jurisprudence, *Mu'amalat* relies primarily on:

- The **Qur'an**, which contains many verses outlining social and economic rules.
- The **Sunnah**, elaborating and clarifying practical applications.
- **Ijma'** (consensus) and **Qiyas** (analogical reasoning) to address new or complex issues.

These sources ensure the law remains rooted in revelation yet adaptable to evolving societal needs.

3. Principles Underpinning Mu'amalat

Key principles include:

- **Justice ('Adl):** Central to all dealings to ensure fairness.

- **Mutual Consent:** Contracts and agreements require the free and informed consent of all parties.

- **Avoidance of Harm (La Darar):** Transactions must not inflict harm or injustice.

- **Good Faith (Ihsan):** Ethical behavior and honesty are mandated.

These principles uphold the moral fabric of Muslim society.

4. Contractual Transactions

Contracts (*'Aqd*) form the backbone of commercial and social dealings.

Fiqh outlines types of contracts including:

- **Sales (Bay'):** Rules on offer, acceptance, price, and conditions.

- **Lease (Ijarah):** Renting agreements with specified terms.

- **Partnerships (Musharakah and Mudarabah):** Investment and profit-sharing frameworks.

- **Loans (Qard):** Loans given without interest, emphasizing repayment and trust.

Validity requires offer, acceptance, lawful subject matter, and clear terms.

5. Prohibition of Riba (Usury/Interest)

A fundamental economic rule is the prohibition of **Riba**, or usury. This prevents exploitation through unjustified increases in loans or trade, protecting social equity and economic justice. The *Fiqh* of

Mu'amalat rigorously defines and prohibits various forms of interest-based transactions.

6. Rules Governing Sales and Trade

Trade is encouraged, but regulated to ensure:

- Transparency and avoidance of deception (*Gharar*).
- Accurate measurement and description of goods.
- Prohibition of forbidden items (e.g., alcohol, pork).
- Restrictions on monopoly and hoarding.

These ensure commerce contributes to societal welfare.

7. Partnership and Investment Models

Islamic finance distinguishes between:

- **Musharakah:** Joint ventures where partners share profits and losses proportionally.
- **Mudarabah:** A contract where one party provides capital and the other manages business.

These models emphasize risk-sharing and ethical profit, contrasting with interest-based finance.

8. Zakat and Economic Justice

Zakat, an obligatory charity, functions within Mu'amalat to redistribute wealth and alleviate poverty. Its administration and collection are guided by detailed rules, reflecting social solidarity.

9. Family Law within Mu'amalat

Marriage, divorce, child custody, and inheritance laws fall under *Mu'amalat* as they regulate personal status and social relations. Shariah prescribes rights and responsibilities for spouses, parents, and heirs to maintain family cohesion.

10. Criminal Law and Hudud

Certain crimes and their punishments are codified within Shariah under *Hudud* laws. While strict, these laws aim to protect societal order and moral standards. The application requires stringent evidentiary standards to prevent injustice.

11. Governance and Public Administration

Islamic political theory and governance principles also form part of *Mu'amalat*. This includes rulers' responsibilities, consultation (*Shura*), justice, and the welfare of the community.

12. Contemporary Applications and Challenges

Modern Muslim societies grapple with applying traditional *Mu'amalat* rulings to complex issues such as:

- Banking and finance in global markets.
- Contractual disputes in secular legal systems.
- Family law reform balancing Shariah and human rights norms.

Scholars engage in Ijtihad to provide contextually relevant solutions.

13. The Role of Ethics and Morality

Ethical considerations permeate all *Mu'amalat* dealings. Islamic jurisprudence insists on sincerity, trustworthiness, and social responsibility beyond mere legal compliance.

14. Preventing Disputes and Encouraging Reconciliation

Fiqh encourages mediation and amicable settlement of disputes. This promotes social harmony and reduces litigation.

15. Mu'amalat and the Objective of Maslahah

Ultimately, *Mu'amalat* aims to secure **Maslahah** (public interest), balancing individual rights with communal welfare. This ensures that social transactions serve the greater good within the framework of divine guidance.

Chapter 20: Fiqh of Family Life

Family life occupies a central place in Islamic jurisprudence, as the family is considered the fundamental unit of society. The *Fiqh* of family life governs the legal, social, and ethical dimensions of familial relationships, outlining rights and responsibilities to ensure harmony, protection, and continuity. Islamic law provides a comprehensive framework addressing marriage, divorce, child custody, inheritance, and related matters, all grounded in the principles of justice, compassion, and social welfare.

1. The Importance of Family in Islam

The family is regarded as the building block of the Muslim community (*Ummah*). It nurtures faith, ethical values, and social cohesion. The Qur'an and Sunnah emphasize the significance of family bonds, highlighting respect for parents, care for children, and mutual responsibilities between spouses.

2. Marriage (Nikah): The Foundation of Family

Marriage in Islam is both a sacred covenant and a legal contract. It aims to establish tranquility, love, and mutual support between spouses.

The *Fiqh* of marriage addresses:

- **Conditions and pillars:** including offer (*Ijab*), acceptance (*Qabul*), consent, and presence of witnesses.
- **Mahr (dowry):** a mandatory gift from the husband to the wife as a symbol of commitment.
- **Eligibility and prohibitions:** such as consanguinity and existing marital status.

- **Rights and duties:** spouses have reciprocal obligations, including maintenance, companionship, and kindness.

3. Polygyny and Its Regulation

Islam permits a man to marry up to four wives under specific conditions. The *Fiqh* stresses:

- **Justice and equal treatment:** between wives in financial and emotional support.

- **Limitations:** men are encouraged toward monogamy if justice cannot be ensured.

- **Social and ethical considerations:** emphasizing responsibility and fairness.

4. Guardianship and Consent in Marriage

In traditional jurisprudence, a guardian (*Wali*) plays a crucial role in the marriage contract, particularly for women. The *Fiqh* outlines the guardian's authority to ensure suitability and protect the bride's interests, balanced with the bride's right to consent.

5. Divorce (Talaq) and Its Procedures

Divorce is permitted but discouraged, reflecting Islam's preference for family stability.

Fiqh defines:

- **Types of divorce:** including repudiation (*Talaq*), judicial divorce (*Khula*), and annulment.

- **Conditions and waiting period (*Iddah*):** to allow reconciliation or verify pregnancy.

- **Rights during and after divorce:** including maintenance, custody, and inheritance rights.

- **Reconciliation mechanisms:** promoting mediation and patience before finalizing divorce.

6. Child Custody (Hadanah) and Guardianship

The protection and upbringing of children are paramount. Custody rules prioritize the child's welfare, usually favoring the mother during early years unless she is unfit. Guardianship extends beyond custody, involving financial responsibility and education.

7. Inheritance (Mirath) Laws

Inheritance rules, detailed in the Qur'an, distribute the deceased's estate among relatives. *Fiqh* establishes fixed shares for heirs, including spouses, parents, and children, balancing justice with protection of family wealth.

8. Maintenance (Nafaqah)

Husband's financial responsibility to support his wife and children is a fundamental aspect. Maintenance covers food, clothing, shelter, and other necessities.The wife's right to maintenance continues during marriage and certain periods after divorce.

9. Rights and Duties of Spouses

Spouses are commanded to treat each other with kindness, respect, and equity.

The *Fiqh* addresses:

- Mutual consultation (*Shura*).

- Sexual rights and responsibilities.
- Prohibition of harm and abuse.
- Shared obligations in managing household affairs.

10. Custodial Rights and Visitation After Divorce

While custody often remains with the mother initially, fathers retain visitation rights. *Fiqh* encourages maintaining family ties despite separation.

11. Marriage of Non-Muslims and Interfaith Considerations

Islamic law regulates marriages involving non-Muslims:

- Muslim men may marry chaste women from the People of the Book.
- Muslim women's marriage to non-Muslims is generally prohibited.
- The status of children and religious upbringing is considered.

12. Adoption and Guardianship

While adoption as traditionally practiced is not recognized in the sense of changing lineage, guardianship (*Kafalah*) is encouraged to care for orphans and needy children. *Fiqh* outlines the rights and responsibilities of guardians without altering the child's family identity.

13. Marriage Contracts and Customary Practices

Contracts may include stipulations agreed upon by spouses, such as living arrangements or financial rights, provided they do not contradict Islamic principles. Customary practices (*Urf*) influence how families implement legal rulings.

14. Protection Against Domestic Violence

Islamic teachings strictly prohibit harm and abuse within the family. *Fiqh* supports the protection of spouses and children, emphasizing mercy and compassion.

15. Legal Reforms and Contemporary Challenges

Modern Muslim societies address evolving family dynamics by engaging with classical *Fiqh* rulings, often seeking balance between tradition and contemporary human rights discourse.

Chapter 21: Fiqh of Crime and Punishment

The *Fiqh* of crime and punishment, known as **'Uqubat**, constitutes a significant domain of Islamic jurisprudence, concerned with maintaining public order, justice, and moral rectitude. It regulates offenses, prescribes penalties, and establishes procedures for adjudication, ensuring that the rights of individuals and society are preserved under the principles of Shariah. This branch reflects the balance between mercy and justice inherent in Islamic law.

1. Objectives of Criminal Law in Islam

Islamic criminal law aims to:

- Protect the faith, life, intellect, lineage, and property.
- Prevent harm and corruption (*Fasad*) in society.
- Uphold justice while safeguarding human dignity.
- Deter crime through appropriate sanctions.
- Provide avenues for repentance and rehabilitation.

These objectives align with the higher purposes (*Maqasid*) of Shariah.

2. Classification of Crimes

Crimes under Islamic law are classified mainly into three categories:

- **Hudud (Fixed Punishments):** Offenses with fixed, divine penalties specified in the Qur'an and Sunnah, such as theft, adultery, apostasy, and false accusation.

- **Qisas (Retaliation):** Crimes involving bodily harm or murder, where the victim or heirs may demand equivalent retribution or forgiveness.

- **Tazir (Discretionary Punishments):** Crimes not covered by Hudud or Qisas, where the judge exercises discretion in sentencing based on the severity and circumstances.

3. Hudud Offenses and Their Rulings

Hudud crimes have strict evidentiary requirements and fixed punishments, including:

- **Theft (*Sariqa*):** Punished by amputation of the hand if conditions such as minimum value and secure possession are met.

- **Adultery (*Zina*):** Punishable by flogging or stoning depending on marital status, requiring stringent proof through confession or witnesses.

- **False Accusation (*Qadhf*):** Penalized by flogging to protect honor.

- **Consumption of Alcohol:** Flogged to deter intoxication.

- **Highway Robbery (*Hirabah*):** Punished variably with execution, crucifixion, or exile depending on severity.

The strict evidentiary standards protect against wrongful conviction.

4. Qisas: Law of Retaliation

Qisas applies to intentional bodily harm and murder.

- The principle is "an eye for an eye," allowing the victim or heirs to demand equal retribution.

- Alternatively, they may forgive or accept compensation (*Diyya*).

- This system promotes justice balanced with mercy and reconciliation.

5. Tazir: Judicial Discretion

Tazir crimes encompass a wide range of offenses, including bribery, slander, or minor theft. Punishments are not fixed and may include imprisonment, fines, corporal punishment, or warnings. Judges consider context, intent, and social impact when deciding penalties.

6. Procedural Safeguards and Evidentiary Rules

Islamic criminal jurisprudence enforces rigorous procedural rules:

- **Proof standards:** Require multiple reliable witnesses or confessions.

- **Presumption of innocence:** Protecting defendants from arbitrary punishment.

- **Prohibition of torture or coerced confession.**

- **Right to defense and fair trial.**

These safeguards uphold justice and prevent abuse.

7. The Role of Repentance and Forgiveness

Islam emphasizes mercy, encouraging repentance (*Tawbah*) and forgiveness.

- Forgiveness by victims can lead to mitigation or abolition of punishments, especially in Qisas cases.

- The state may also exercise clemency, reflecting the compassionate nature of Islamic law.

8. Capital Punishment

Execution is prescribed for severe offenses such as intentional murder and certain Hudud crimes. It is carried out under strict procedural requirements to prevent miscarriages of justice. Islamic law regards capital punishment as a last resort to protect societal welfare.

9. Juveniles and the Mentally Incapacitated

Islamic jurisprudence exempts children below maturity and those lacking mental capacity from criminal liability. This reflects the principle of justice and personal accountability.

10. Punishment and Reform

Islamic criminal law seeks not only to punish but also to reform the offender. Corrective measures, education, and reintegration into society are encouraged wherever possible.

11. Contemporary Challenges

Modern Muslim states face challenges in applying classical *Fiqh* of crime and punishment, especially concerning human rights, due process, and international law. Scholars and jurists engage in *Ijtihad* to reconcile traditional rulings with contemporary standards.

12. The State's Role and Public Interest

The enforcement of criminal law is primarily the responsibility of the state. The state acts as the guardian of public interest (*Maslahah*), ensuring laws serve societal welfare while respecting individual rights.

Chapter 22: Fiqh of Governance and Public Policy

The *Fiqh* of governance and public policy, known in Islamic jurisprudence as the regulation of political authority and communal affairs, forms a crucial aspect of Shariah. It addresses the principles, structures, and responsibilities involved in leading a Muslim society in accordance with divine guidance. This branch reflects Islam's comprehensive approach to not only individual and social ethics but also collective leadership, justice, and welfare.

1. The Concept of Governance in Islam

Islamic governance is centered on the concept of **Shura** (consultation), **Adl** (justice), and **Maslahah** (public interest). Governance is viewed as a trust (*Amanah*) bestowed upon rulers, who must act in accordance with the Qur'an, Sunnah, and the welfare of the people.

2. The Role and Legitimacy of the Ruler

The ruler (*Imam* or *Khalifah*) holds authority derived from the consent of the governed and divine mandate. Legitimacy depends on adherence to Shariah, ensuring justice, and protecting the community.

3. Consultation (Shura) as a Governance Principle

The Qur'an enjoins Muslims to decide matters by mutual consultation. *Fiqh* prescribes mechanisms for leaders to consult knowledgeable and representative members of society, fostering inclusive decision-making.

4. Justice (Adl) as the Foundation of Public Policy

Justice is paramount in governance. Rulers must uphold fairness in law enforcement, economic distribution, and protection of rights, reflecting Quranic injunctions.

5. The Concept of Maslahah (Public Interest)

Policies must promote the welfare of the community. Maslahah serves as a guiding principle for legislative and administrative decisions, balancing individual and collective needs.

6. The Role of Accountability

Islamic governance emphasizes the accountability of rulers to the people and ultimately to Allah. Corruption, oppression, or neglect of duties are condemned.

7. The Administration of Justice

The judicial system operates independently to uphold Shariah. Judges (*Qadis*) are appointed based on knowledge and integrity, ensuring fair trials and dispute resolution.

8. Public Welfare and Social Justice

Governance entails ensuring social justice, including poverty alleviation, education, health, and equitable resource distribution. State responsibility extends to protecting vulnerable groups.

9. Economic Policy and Regulation

The state regulates economic activities to prevent exploitation, ensure ethical trade, and promote equitable growth. Zakat collection and distribution are part of public policy to address poverty.

10. Defense and Security

Protecting the community from external and internal threats is a fundamental duty. The state organizes defense and maintains public order while respecting rights.

11. Religious Freedom and Minority Rights

Islamic governance recognizes the rights of religious minorities under the *Dhimmi* system, ensuring protection and freedom to practice their faith within legal frameworks.

12. Role of Law Enforcement

The enforcement of laws involves agencies acting within ethical boundaries. Punishments and regulations are implemented with due process and respect for human dignity.

13. Governance in the Absence of a Central Authority

Islamic jurisprudence addresses leadership and governance in times of political fragmentation, emphasizing community consensus and local administration.

14. Contemporary Application and Reform

Modern Muslim states adapt classical principles to contemporary governance challenges, including constitutionalism, democracy, and human rights. *Ijtihad* plays a role in contextualizing public policy.

15. The Ethical Dimension of Leadership

Leaders are expected to embody moral virtues such as honesty, humility, and service. Ethical governance is critical for legitimacy and social harmony.

Chapter 23: Colonialism and the Decline of Sharia Implementation

The advent of European colonialism in Muslim lands from the 18th century onward marked a significant turning point in the history of Islamic law (*Shariah*) implementation. The imposition of foreign political, legal, and administrative systems undermined traditional Islamic governance and jurisprudence, leading to profound transformations in Muslim societies. This chapter explores the dynamics of colonial influence on the application of *Fiqh*, the challenges faced by Muslim jurists, and the legacy of this period.

1. The Expansion of European Colonial Powers

European powers, notably Britain, France, and later others, expanded their control over large Muslim-majority territories in Asia, Africa, and the Middle East. Colonial administration sought to restructure governance, often sidelining Islamic legal institutions.

2. Displacement of Islamic Legal Systems

Colonial regimes introduced secular legal codes based on European models, often French civil law or British common law, supplanting *Shariah*-based courts and laws. This resulted in the marginalization of Islamic jurisprudence, particularly in criminal and commercial law.

3. Impact on Judicial Authority

Traditional *Qadis* and religious scholars saw their authority diminished as colonial courts became dominant. The colonial legal system often disregarded Islamic legal principles, causing confusion and loss of confidence among Muslim populations.

4. The Role of Colonial Legal Pluralism

In some regions, colonial powers allowed limited application of Islamic law in personal status matters such as marriage, divorce, and inheritance, to avoid social unrest. This created a dual legal system but limited *Shariah* to private law domains.

5. Transformation of Islamic Education and Scholarship

Colonialism affected Islamic institutions (*madaris* and *al-Azhar*) by reducing funding and influence. Western education and legal philosophies challenged traditional Islamic sciences, leading to intellectual tensions.

6. Responses of Muslim Jurists and Reformers

Many Muslim scholars sought to defend and revive *Shariah* within the constraints imposed. Reform movements emerged, aiming to reconcile Islamic law with modernity, sometimes advocating selective adoption of Western legal concepts.

7. Codification Efforts and Legal Modernization

Some Muslim-majority states undertook codification of family and commercial laws inspired by European models but often incorporating Islamic principles. These codifications represented both adaptation and limitation of classical *Fiqh*.

8. Colonial Policies and the Control of Religious Authorities

Colonial powers co-opted religious leaders to legitimize their rule, sometimes undermining genuine Islamic authority. This politicization altered the traditional role of *Ulama* in jurisprudence and governance.

9. Economic and Social Consequences

The colonial imposition disrupted traditional economic systems governed by Islamic principles, affecting zakat, waqf, and charitable institutions. Social stratification deepened, impacting access to justice and legal remedies.

10. The Rise of Nationalist Movements

Anti-colonial movements often invoked Islamic identity and Shariah as symbols of resistance and social justice. These movements sought to reclaim Islamic law's role in post-colonial nation-building.

11. Legacy of Colonial Legal Systems Post-Independence

After independence, many Muslim countries retained elements of colonial legal frameworks. The challenge became how to reintegrate Islamic law within modern state structures and international norms.

12. Contemporary Debates on Shariah and Legal Pluralism

The colonial legacy informs ongoing debates about the scope and nature of *Shariah* in modern legal systems, balancing tradition and pluralism.

Chapter 24: Modernists vs. Traditionalists

The encounter between Islamic tradition and modernity has generated significant intellectual and practical debates among Muslim scholars and communities. This tension is often framed as a discourse between *Modernists* and *Traditionalists*, reflecting differing approaches to Islamic jurisprudence (*Fiqh*) and theology (*Aqeedah*) in the contemporary world. This chapter explores the origins, arguments, and impact of these perspectives within the ongoing effort to define Islam's place in modern society.

1. Historical Context of the Divide

The 19th and 20th centuries witnessed dramatic political, social, and intellectual changes in Muslim lands, largely shaped by colonialism, modernization, and Western influence. This context catalyzed divergent responses regarding the interpretation and application of Islamic law and creed.

2. The Modernist Movement: Reform and Adaptation

Modernists advocated for a critical re-examination of Islamic texts to harmonize Islam with contemporary knowledge, science, and political realities. Key figures such as Jamal al-Din al-Afghani, Muhammad Abduh, and Rashid Rida emphasized:

- Rationalism and ijtihad (independent reasoning) over taqlid (blind adherence to tradition).
- Reforming *Fiqh* to address modern social, economic, and political needs.
- Reconciling Islam with democracy, human rights, and education.

- Rejecting superstition and literalist interpretations that hinder progress.

3. Traditionalist Perspective: Preservation of Orthodoxy

Traditionalists stressed the continuity and authority of established Islamic jurisprudence and theology.They upheld:

- The primacy of classical *Madhahib* (legal schools) and established theological creeds.

- Caution against excessive reinterpretation that might compromise authenticity.

- Adherence to the consensus (*Ijma'*) of scholars and respect for inherited methodologies.

- Emphasis on preserving spiritual, ethical, and ritual dimensions of Islam.

4. Points of Contention

The divide often revolves around:

- The scope and legitimacy of *ijtihad* in the modern era.

- The application of Shariah in state law versus private spheres.

- Gender roles, family law, and social reforms.

- Engagement with Western philosophy and secularism.

5. Modernist Approaches to Legal Reform

Modernists pushed for:

- Revising family laws to improve women's rights.
- Incorporating modern finance and commercial codes.
- Establishing constitutional frameworks consistent with Islamic principles.
- Utilizing maqasid al-Shariah (objectives of Islamic law) for legal interpretation.

6. Traditionalist Defense of Classical Jurisprudence

Traditionalists argue:

- Classical *Fiqh* is sufficiently flexible to address new issues.
- Reforms should occur within established frameworks.
- Innovations risk fragmenting Muslim unity and compromising religious integrity.

7. Educational and Institutional Differences

Modernists often advocate reforming Islamic education to include secular subjects and critical thinking. Traditionalists maintain classical curricula focused on memorization and transmission of traditional texts.

8. Impact on Muslim Societies

These intellectual currents influence legal codes, political movements, and social policies across the Muslim world. Conflicts between modernist-inspired reforms and traditionalist resistance continue to shape public discourse.

9. Hybrid and Middle Approaches

Some scholars seek synthesis, combining respect for tradition with contextual adaptation. This approach aims to bridge gaps and provide balanced frameworks for contemporary challenges.

10. Role of Globalization and Technology

The information age amplifies these debates, enabling widespread dissemination of diverse views and fostering dialogue and contestation.

11. Gender and Social Issues

Modernist critiques have led to re-examinations of women's rights, education, and participation in public life. Traditionalists often emphasize preserving established roles while encouraging education within Islamic bounds.

12. Political Implications

Modernist and traditionalist visions influence Islamist movements, state policies, and inter-community relations, often impacting governance models.

13. Future Prospects

Ongoing interaction between modernist and traditionalist perspectives shapes the evolving understanding of Islam's role in the modern world.

Chapter 25: Salafism and the Literalist Revival

Salafism represents a significant movement within contemporary Islamic thought, marked by a call to return to the practices and beliefs of the *Salaf*—the pious predecessors, particularly the first three generations of Muslims. This chapter examines the emergence of Salafism, its emphasis on textual literalism, its impact on Islamic jurisprudence and creed, and its role in modern Muslim societies.

1. Historical Origins of Salafism

The term *Salaf* refers to the early generations of Muslims deemed exemplary in faith and practice. While adherence to the *Salaf* has always been a feature of Sunni Islam, the modern Salafi movement crystallized in the late 19th and early 20th centuries as a response to colonialism, religious innovation (*bid'ah*), and perceived decline in Muslim religiosity.

2. Key Figures and Early Influences

Early reformers like Muhammad ibn Abd al-Wahhab in the Arabian Peninsula championed a puritanical return to the Qur'an and Sunnah, rejecting later theological and jurisprudential developments they saw as deviations. This movement stressed strict monotheism (*Tawhid*) and eradication of practices considered innovations or superstitions.

3. Core Doctrines of Salafism

Salafism is characterized by:

- Literalist interpretation of the Qur'an and Hadith.
- Rejection of theological speculation (*Kalam*).
- Opposition to *Taqlid* (blind following) of later jurists, advocating for direct engagement with primary texts.

- Strict adherence to the apparent meanings of texts without metaphorical interpretation.

- Emphasis on *Aqeedah* free from philosophical or mystical influences.

4. Salafism and Islamic Jurisprudence

Salafi jurists often adopt a scripturalist approach, prioritizing the texts of the Qur'an and Sunnah over the traditional schools (*Madhahib*). This leads to selective acceptance or rejection of classical jurisprudence, aiming to derive rulings based on clear textual evidence.

5. The Literalist Approach to Theology

Salafism rejects speculative theology and philosophical theology (*Ilm al-Kalam*), focusing instead on affirming the divine attributes as stated in scripture, without metaphorical interpretation. This distinguishes Salafism from Ash'ari and Maturidi theological schools.

6. Salafi Methodology and Criteria for Authenticity

The movement places great emphasis on the authenticity and soundness of Hadith. Only rigorously authenticated texts are used as the basis for belief and law.

7. Salafism's Stance on Sufism and Popular Practices

Salafism generally rejects Sufi practices such as saint veneration and certain forms of devotional acts, labeling them as innovations or polytheistic. This position often leads to tensions with traditional Sufi communities.

8. Political Dimensions of Salafism

Salafism includes diverse strands: quietist, activist, and jihadist. While some Salafis focus on personal piety and avoiding politics, others engage in political activism or militancy, aiming to establish governance based on Salafi interpretations.

9. Spread and Influence in the Modern World

Saudi Arabia and other Gulf states have been instrumental in spreading Salafi teachings globally through funding, education, and media. This has led to the movement's significant presence across various Muslim communities worldwide.

10. Critiques and Controversies

Salafism faces criticism for its perceived rigidity, intolerance toward differing interpretations, and sometimes confrontational approach to Muslim diversity. Critics argue it oversimplifies complex jurisprudential and theological issues.

11. Relationship with Other Islamic Movements

Salafism often opposes both traditionalist scholars and modernist reformers, positioning itself as a distinct path. Its literalism contrasts with both the methodological flexibility of traditional schools and the rationalism of modernists.

12. Salafism and Contemporary Islamic Law

Salafi jurists advocate for a return to *Fiqh* derived solely from clear scriptural sources, often rejecting later juristic consensus when deemed inconsistent with texts. This affects interpretations in worship, social issues, and governance.

13. Educational and Social Outreach

Salafism invests heavily in education through *madrasas*, publications, and online platforms, promoting its approach to a broad audience.

14. The Movement's Impact on Muslim Identity

Salafism influences debates about authenticity, religious authority, and community boundaries in the modern Muslim world.

Chapter 26: The Rise of Political Islam

The twentieth century witnessed a profound transformation in the relationship between Islam and politics, marked by the emergence of Political Islam (*Islamism*) as a significant ideological and social force. This chapter explores the origins, development, and characteristics of Political Islam, tracing its diverse manifestations and impact on Muslim societies and global politics.

1. Historical Background and Early Influences

Political Islam arose partly in response to colonialism, Western dominance, and the decline of traditional Islamic governance. Early 20th-century thinkers like Hassan al-Banna and Sayyid Qutb laid the intellectual groundwork by advocating for the reintegration of Islam into political life and society.

2. The Founding of the Muslim Brotherhood

Founded in Egypt in 1928 by Hassan al-Banna, the Muslim Brotherhood became the prototype of organized Political Islam. It emphasized social reform, education, charity, and ultimately political activism grounded in Islamic principles.

3. Ideological Foundations

Political Islam asserts that Islam is a comprehensive system governing all aspects of life, including governance, law, economy, and morality. It rejects the secular separation of religion and state, advocating for the implementation of Shariah as the legal and political framework.

4. Key Concepts: Ummah, Hakimiyyah, and Jihad

- *Ummah* (Muslim community) is central, emphasizing unity under Islamic law.

- *Hakimiyyah* refers to the sovereignty of God as the ultimate authority, rejecting human-made legislation that contradicts divine law.

- *Jihad* is framed variably as spiritual struggle or political resistance against oppression.

5. Varied Currents within Political Islam

Political Islam is not monolithic; it includes:

- Moderate reformists seeking gradual change via political participation.

- Radical groups advocating revolutionary overthrow of existing regimes.

- Militants who endorse armed struggle.

6. Political Islam in Post-Colonial States

Many post-independence Muslim-majority countries faced challenges of nation-building, authoritarianism, and socio-economic disparity. Political Islam often emerged as opposition to secular regimes perceived as corrupt or Westernized.

7. Interaction with Secular Nationalism and Leftist Movements

Political Islam often conflicted with secular nationalist and socialist ideologies dominating post-colonial politics. At times, alliances were formed, but deep ideological differences persisted.

8. State Responses to Political Islam

Governments varied in their response, ranging from repression and bans to co-optation and incorporation into political systems. The oscillation shaped the movement's strategies and public image.

9. The Iranian Revolution: A Milestone

The 1979 Iranian Revolution marked a watershed, establishing an Islamic Republic governed by Shia clerical authority. It inspired both hope and apprehension among Sunni and Shia Muslims regarding Islamic governance.

10. The Role of Political Islam in Global Conflicts

Political Islam has intersected with regional conflicts, such as in Palestine, Afghanistan, and Syria, influencing resistance movements and foreign policy.

11. Political Islam and Democracy

Debates persist regarding compatibility between Islamic governance and democratic principles. Some Islamist parties participate in elections, while others reject democratic legitimacy.

12. Women and Political Islam

Political Islam's stance on gender roles varies, with some advocating for traditional roles and others encouraging women's political participation within Islamic frameworks.

13. Media, Technology, and Political Islam

The rise of satellite TV, internet, and social media has amplified Political Islam's reach and influence globally.

14. Challenges and Criticisms

Critiques include accusations of intolerance, authoritarian tendencies, and failure to address pluralism and human rights adequately.

15. The Future Trajectory

Political Islam continues to evolve amid global political shifts, internal debates, and generational changes within Muslim societies.

Chapter 27: Contemporary Ijtihad and Fiqh Councils

In the face of complex modern realities, the traditional mechanism of *ijtihad*—independent legal reasoning—has experienced a revival. This resurgence has been guided and institutionalized by various *Fiqh* councils across the Muslim world and within diaspora communities. These councils seek to address new challenges while maintaining fidelity to Islamic legal and ethical frameworks.

1. The Reopening of Ijtihad

Historically, the gates of *ijtihad* were considered by some to have closed after the formative centuries of Islamic jurisprudence. However, contemporary conditions—scientific advancements, global interconnectivity, political change, and the emergence of Muslim minorities in non-Muslim lands—have prompted renewed scholarly consensus on the need for qualified *ijtihad*.

2. Criteria for Contemporary Mujtahids

Modern scholars capable of performing *ijtihad* are expected to master:

- Arabic language and rhetoric.
- The Qur'an and the Sunnah in both content and context.
- Principles of *Usul al-Fiqh* (legal theory).
- Knowledge of maqasid al-Shari'ah (objectives of Islamic law).
- Familiarity with the classical schools of jurisprudence and the socio-cultural realities of the modern world.

These qualifications are typically found in scholars working collectively rather than individually, which has led to the formation of institutional bodies.

3. Emergence of Fiqh Councils

In response to the demands of the global Muslim population, various international and regional *Fiqh* councils have emerged, such as:

- The International Islamic Fiqh Academy (IIFA) under the Organization of Islamic Cooperation.
- The European Council for Fatwa and Research.
- The Fiqh Council of North America.
- The Islamic Fiqh Academy of India.
- Dar al-Ifta institutions in Egypt, Jordan, and elsewhere.

These bodies aim to provide scholarly, collective deliberation on contemporary issues by combining classical jurisprudence with modern methodologies.

4. Methodology and Process

Fiqh councils utilize *ijtihad jama'i*—collective legal reasoning. This process includes:

- Gathering specialists in different disciplines, including economics, medicine, and social sciences.
- Reviewing scriptural sources alongside modern data.
- Ensuring that fatwas and resolutions respect both traditional jurisprudential methods and local context.

This multi-disciplinary approach reflects an expansion of the classical *ijtihad* model to accommodate the breadth of contemporary concerns.

5. Issues Addressed by Contemporary Ijtihad

Contemporary *Fiqh* councils have issued fatwas and legal opinions on a wide range of issues including:

- Bioethics: organ donation, fertility treatments, genetic engineering, and euthanasia.

- Finance: Islamic banking, digital currency, zakat on stocks, and insurance.

- Technology: artificial intelligence, surveillance, and data privacy.

- Social matters: gender roles, family law, citizenship, and minority rights.

- Environment: Islamic perspectives on climate change, pollution, and conservation.

These rulings are often context-sensitive, distinguishing between rulings for Muslims in Muslim-majority states and those living as minorities in secular or non-Muslim countries.

6. Minority Fiqh (Fiqh al-Aqalliyyat)

One of the most significant developments in modern *ijtihad* is the emergence of *Fiqh al-Aqalliyyat*—jurisprudence for Muslim minorities. It addresses questions of religious practice, integration, and identity, offering solutions that balance adherence to Islamic law with the legal and cultural environment of non-Muslim societies. This area of *Fiqh* has produced flexible rulings on participation in democratic elections, use of conventional finance in certain contexts, and concessions in religious observance under constraints.

7. The Role of Maqasid al-Shariah

Modern *ijtihad* increasingly relies on the higher objectives of Islamic law (*maqasid*), including the preservation of religion, life, intellect, lineage, and wealth. This framework allows scholars to prioritize values and outcomes over literalist application, especially in unprecedented or multifaceted cases. The elevation of *maqasid* supports dynamic jurisprudence while maintaining consistency with core Islamic values.

8. Challenges Facing Contemporary Ijtihad

Fiqh councils face a number of obstacles, including:

- Divergence in national and ideological perspectives.
- Tensions between traditionalist and reformist scholars.
- Pressure from governments or interest groups.
- The rapid pace of technological change.
- Skepticism from lay Muslims regarding the authority and applicability of modern rulings.

Despite these challenges, the institutionalization of *ijtihad* remains a critical development in the evolution of Islamic legal thought.

Chapter 28: Women and Modern Fiqh

The role of women in Islam has long been a subject of legal, cultural, and theological discussion. In the modern era, shifting social landscapes and global discourse on gender equality have intensified scrutiny of women's legal status within Islamic jurisprudence. Contemporary fiqh scholars have reexamined traditional rulings through the lenses of *ijtihad*, *maqasid al-shariah*, and lived realities, offering nuanced perspectives on gender roles, rights, and obligations.

1. Revisiting Foundational Texts

Early Islamic sources—primarily the Qur'an and Hadith—contain numerous references to women's spiritual, social, and legal status. While these texts were historically interpreted in patriarchal societies, modern scholars emphasize a contextual reading that distinguishes between foundational principles and time-bound applications. Legal rulings concerning women in areas such as inheritance, testimony, and dress code have been subjects of re-analysis in light of both classical juristic discourse and modern social developments.

2. Education and Public Participation

Historically, women in the early Islamic period played active roles in education and public life. Aisha bint Abi Bakr, for example, was a prominent transmitter of Hadith and a jurist. Contemporary scholars have revisited this legacy to support women's access to higher education, religious scholarship, and civic participation.

Modern fiqh councils have ruled that there is no legal impediment for women to serve as educators, judges, and members of public office, provided the conditions of modesty, qualification, and public interest are upheld.

3. Women's Dress and Modesty (Hijab and Beyond)

Legal discussions surrounding women's dress, particularly hijab, have evolved to include questions about agency, cultural expression, and professional obligations. While the obligation of modest dress is affirmed in traditional rulings, the interpretation of what constitutes hijab varies across legal schools and cultural contexts.

Modern jurists debate whether the face veil (niqab) is obligatory, recommended, or culturally specific. Some argue that emphasizing ethical modesty and intention should take precedence over rigid uniformity.

4. Marriage, Consent, and Guardianship

One of the most discussed topics in modern fiqh regarding women is the structure of marriage contracts. The principle of *wali* (guardian) is reexamined, especially in non-Muslim countries where civil law requires personal consent without guardianship.

Scholars in the minority fiqh discourse have allowed for adult women to enter into marriage contracts without a guardian under certain conditions, emphasizing autonomy and the requirement of mutual consent, as validated by Prophetic traditions.

5. Polygamy and Its Contemporary Relevance

While polygamy is permitted in Islamic law, contemporary scholars have scrutinized its application in modern societies. Fiqh councils increasingly emphasize the Qur'anic condition of justice between wives as a practical limitation rather than a formal one.

Legal frameworks in some Muslim-majority countries now require the consent of the first wife or judicial review, reflecting a shift toward curbing misuse and aligning with the *maqasid* of family stability and fairness.

6. Divorce and Custody

Modern fiqh places greater emphasis on women's rights in initiating divorce (*khula*) and securing equitable treatment in post-divorce arrangements. Access to Islamic courts, clear documentation of financial rights (*mahr* and maintenance), and fair child custody have become areas of reform.

Custody rulings are increasingly based on the best interest of the child rather than rigid age-based thresholds, and mothers are often given priority, particularly in early developmental years.

7. Economic Rights and Property Ownership

Islam granted women the right to own, inherit, and manage wealth independently—a radical concept in its early context. Contemporary application has sought to reinforce these rights, especially in cultures where patriarchal customs override religious mandates.

Women today engage in commerce, entrepreneurship, and finance in accordance with Islamic legal principles. Scholars have clarified that participation in economic life does not compromise modesty or religiosity.

8. Participation in Religious Leadership

Although the role of women as imams in mixed congregations remains a contested issue, many scholars allow for women to lead other women in prayer, deliver educational lectures, and issue religious guidance.

Institutions such as Al-Azhar and various Western Islamic centers have trained female muftis and chaplains, recognizing their role in addressing the spiritual and legal needs of Muslim women.

9. Women in Fiqh Councils and Scholarly Circles

Contemporary fiqh councils increasingly include female scholars, particularly in regions like North America, Europe, and Southeast Asia. Their participation enriches legal discourse by providing perspectives grounded in women's lived experiences and scholarly expertise. The integration of female voices into the legal process has led to more balanced fatwas on issues ranging from reproductive ethics to family law.

10. Reproductive Ethics and Medical Issues

Modern fiqh has tackled complex issues such as contraception, fertility treatment, menstrual health, and abortion. Consensus generally permits contraception within marriage if agreed upon by both spouses. Fertility treatments are allowed if no third-party genetic material is used. Abortion rulings vary, with most scholars permitting it only within 120 days under strict conditions. The evolving field of biomedical ethics continues to shape Islamic perspectives on women's health.

Chapter 29: Fiqh of Minorities (Fiqh al-Aqalliyat)

As global migration patterns shifted and Muslim populations established permanent residence in non-Muslim-majority countries, a distinct branch of Islamic jurisprudence known as *Fiqh al-Aqalliyat*—the jurisprudence of Muslim minorities—emerged to address the unique challenges of practicing Islam in secular or pluralistic societies. This legal development operates within the traditional frameworks of *usul al-fiqh* while responding to sociopolitical conditions unfamiliar to earlier jurists.

1. Historical Precedents and Theoretical Roots

While the term *Fiqh al-Aqalliyat* is relatively new, its foundations are traceable to early Islamic history. The emigration of Muslims to Abyssinia during the lifetime of the Prophet (pbuh), under the protection of a non-Muslim king, serves as a precedent for coexistence under foreign rule. Classical jurists also addressed the legal status of Muslims residing in *Dar al-Harb* (non-Muslim lands) or *Dar al-'Ahd* (lands with treaties), formulating guidelines on religious obligations, interactions, and allegiances. Modern interpretations rely heavily on *maqasid al-shari'ah* (the objectives of Islamic law) to evaluate rulings in non-Muslim contexts, ensuring the preservation of religion, life, intellect, lineage, and property.

2. Juristic Adaptation to Secular Environments

Fiqh councils and minority scholars assess whether traditional rulings need adaptation due to social constraints or legal obligations imposed by secular governments. These adaptations do not compromise core religious principles but aim to provide flexibility in application.

Examples include adjusting prayer times in regions with extreme daylight cycles, allowing participation in non-Islamic financial systems with safeguards, or permitting interest-based mortgages in certain cases where no halal alternatives exist and the need is pressing.

3. Citizenship and Political Engagement

Muslim minorities often live as full citizens in democratic societies, raising questions of loyalty, political participation, and national service. Contemporary *fiqh* views participation in democratic elections as not only permissible but, in some cases, encouraged—particularly when such participation can protect community interests and prevent harm.

Naturalization and military service are permitted when they do not entail direct involvement in injustice. Loyalty to the state is distinguished from theological allegiance, with emphasis placed on the principle of covenant and trust (*'ahd*).

4. Interfaith Relations and Social Integration

Interactions with people of other faiths are governed by principles of justice, cooperation, and mutual respect. *Fiqh al-Aqalliyāt* allows for cooperation in civil society, interfaith dialogue, and shared community initiatives so long as they do not compromise religious beliefs or ethics.

Participation in non-Muslim celebrations, for instance, is addressed through nuanced fatwas that weigh the social intent and religious boundaries, differentiating between cultural gestures and religious endorsement.

5. Halal Standards and Dietary Laws

Access to halal food remains a priority. In minority contexts, reliance on certification bodies and broader definitions of halal slaughter have become necessary. Some scholars accept meat from the People of the Book, particularly in cases of difficulty, while others maintain stricter views, reflecting ongoing diversity in jurisprudential approach.

In school systems or institutions where halal options are limited, rulings have supported vegetarian alternatives or temporary exemptions with the intention of preserving religious integrity while avoiding hardship.

6. Islamic Education and Preserving Identity

Maintaining religious identity through education is a central concern in minority settings. Home-based instruction, weekend schools, and Islamic schools have developed to fill the void left by secular curricula. Fiqh deliberations have also addressed permissible content, the integration of secular subjects, and collaboration with public institutions to safeguard both faith and academic excellence.

7. Financial Matters and Riba (Interest)

Economic survival in non-Muslim societies often entails interaction with interest-based financial institutions. *Fiqh al-Aqalliyat* has permitted limited engagement with such systems in the absence of Islamic alternatives, especially for purchasing primary residences or engaging in necessary contracts, based on the principle of necessity (*darurah*) and hardship removal (*raf' al-haraj*). This allowance remains subject to ethical conditions and ongoing efforts to develop independent Islamic financial structures in Western contexts.

8. Gender Interaction and Social Norms

Muslim minorities frequently encounter mixed-gender environments in work, education, and public life. Contemporary rulings recognize the practical realities of such interactions and focus on upholding modesty, intention, and professional conduct, rather than advocating strict segregation. Muslim students and employees are advised to maintain Islamic ethics while respectfully navigating institutional policies and social expectations.

9. Burial and End-of-Life Issues

Fiqh councils have addressed burial rights, autopsy consent, and end-of-life care in jurisdictions where Islamic customs are not recognized. Legal wills, medical directives, and funeral preparations are encouraged to ensure that Muslim rites are observed, and to prevent complications in the absence of community infrastructure. Some councils also address repatriation versus local burial, prioritizing financial feasibility, family wishes, and Islamic guidelines on speed and simplicity of burial.

10. Role of Local Imams and Scholars

Local scholars and imams often serve as the front line of *Fiqh al-Aqalliyat*, balancing scriptural fidelity with cultural sensitivity. Their role includes mediating between classical sources and present-day needs, offering context-based guidance, and preserving unity within diverse communities. These leaders increasingly rely on digital platforms, legal networks, and multilingual resources to deliver responsive, informed religious leadership.

Chapter 30: Aqeedah in the Age of Science and Skepticism

The rise of modern science, global secularism, and post-Enlightenment skepticism has reshaped the intellectual climate in which Islamic theology—*Aqeedah*—must now be articulated. Questions concerning existence, causality, metaphysics, and religious authority are no longer confined to academic circles but permeate popular culture, education, and digital discourse. Muslims living in this era face a unique challenge: maintaining fidelity to *Tawheed* and the established beliefs of Islam while engaging with a world increasingly defined by empiricism and relativism.

1. Epistemological Shifts in Modernity

Classical *Aqeedah* is rooted in a harmonious model of *naql* (revelation) and *'aql* (reason). This synthesis was undermined by the philosophical shift initiated in Europe during the 17th and 18th centuries, which placed sensory perception and empirical verification above metaphysical or revealed knowledge.

The dominance of positivism led many to regard religious beliefs as unverifiable, thus non-rational. Islamic theologians responded by emphasizing the limits of empiricism in addressing existential questions, asserting that revelation complements reason rather than contradicting it.

2. Faith, Proof, and the Nature of Certainty

Islam distinguishes between *yaqeen* (certainty), *zanṇ* (probability), and *shakk* (doubt). The Quran presents *Tawheed* not as a blind commitment but as a truth grounded in signs—*ayat*—in nature, history, and within the self.

Contemporary Muslim theologians emphasize that the existence of God, the need for divine guidance, and the reality of the afterlife lie outside the scope of laboratory-based science. Instead, they rest on rational coherence, moral necessity, and the spiritual intuitions embedded within human nature (*fitrah*). Science, by its method, cannot negate metaphysical truths; it simply does not operate within that register.

3. Cosmology and the Creator

Modern cosmology's revelations about the origins of the universe—such as the Big Bang theory and the fine-tuning of cosmic constants—have prompted renewed theological reflections. Islamic scholars highlight how such discoveries align with Quranic verses describing the heavens and the earth originating from a singularity, and the ordered balance of creation.

While caution is exercised against theological dependence on mutable scientific theories, such developments are utilized to support the Quranic worldview as one that anticipates reflection on the natural world as a path to recognizing the Creator.

4. Evolution, Human Origins, and Divine Purpose

The theory of biological evolution presents one of the most debated intersections between science and *Aqeedah*. Classical Islamic belief holds that Adam ('alayhi as-salam) was a uniquely created being, not descended from earlier life forms. However, the broader theory of evolution in the non-human domain has been addressed with greater openness.

Islamic scholars have differentiated between methodological naturalism—science working within natural laws—and philosophical naturalism, which denies the need for a creator. It is the latter that conflicts with Islamic theology, not the scientific process itself.

5. Secularism and the Marginalization of God

Secular modernity has not merely removed God from scientific inquiry but has marginalized the Divine from public life and ethical discourse. This relegation challenges the traditional Islamic view, where *Aqeedah* forms the center of personal, legal, and social life.

In response, Muslims advocate for a reorientation of knowledge grounded in *Tawheed*, where divine purpose and accountability frame one's understanding of the world. This is not a rejection of secular tools but a refusal to adopt a worldview that denies transcendence.

6. Moral Relativism and the Collapse of Absolutes

In a postmodern context, belief in objective truth is often replaced by individual experience as the sole arbiter of morality. Islamic *Aqeedah*, by contrast, is built on the premise that truth is singular and that values are grounded in divine revelation.

This has significant implications for bioethics, gender identity, and human rights, where Muslims are increasingly required to articulate their positions in societies that reject fixed moral frameworks. Islamic theology reasserts that divine guidance is not oppressive but protective, preserving human dignity and social order.

7. Digital Age and Doubt Culture

The internet has enabled instant access to information but also the proliferation of doubt, confusion, and ideological manipulation. Online platforms often present decontextualized critiques of Islam, leading some to intellectual or spiritual disorientation.

Contemporary scholars and thinkers have emphasized the need for structured *Tarbiyah* (spiritual and intellectual development), critical thinking skills, and rootedness in traditional knowledge to build resilience against these ideological currents.

8. Revival of Theological Discourse

The response to scientific and philosophical skepticism has not been a retreat into fideism but a revival of systematic theology rooted in the Quran, Sunnah, and rational inquiry. Thinkers in institutions across the Muslim world and the West are producing new kalam literature, drawing from classical sources while addressing modern dilemmas.

Topics such as the problem of evil, consciousness, divine will, and freedom are now engaged using both traditional frameworks and contemporary philosophical language, offering a rich and evolving intellectual tradition.

Chapter 31: Tasawwuf and the Inner Dimensions of Fiqh and Aqeedah

In the Islamic tradition, **Tasawwuf** represents the spiritual path toward inner purification and the experiential realization of divine presence. This chapter examines how Sufism enriches the practical application of fiqh and deepens the understanding of aqeedah, emphasizing that outer legal and doctrinal precision must be complemented by the transformation of the soul.

1. The Spiritual Significance of Tasawwuf

Tasawwuf engages with the human heart and consciousness, aiming to cleanse it from the vices of pride, greed, and heedlessness. The inner journey involves cultivating virtues such as humility, sincerity, and love for Allah. Sufi practices—including regular remembrance (*dhikr*), meditation, and moral self-discipline—are designed to awaken latent spiritual faculties and align the individual with divine reality. This internal transformation is regarded as essential for the proper external observance of religious duties.

2. Integration of Tasawwuf with Fiqh

While classical fiqh provides detailed guidelines for rituals and ethical conduct, it primarily addresses the external aspects of religious observance. Tasawwuf offers a complementary perspective that ensures actions are performed with genuine consciousness and heartfelt devotion. In this integrated model, the letter of the law is infused with the spirit of worship. For example, the discipline required in performing the daily prayers (*salah*) is augmented by a focus on the inward state—transforming routine recitation into an act of profound communion with the Divine.

3. Enriching Aqeedah Through Inner Realization

The doctrines of aqeedah, formulated through scriptural texts and scholarly discourse, establish the framework for Islamic belief.

Tasawwuf deepens this framework by encouraging personal experiences that confirm the unseen realities central to faith. Through contemplative practices and the purification of the heart, believers come to perceive the attributes of Allah not merely as abstract tenets but as vivid, lived realities. This experiential knowledge reinforces doctrinal conviction and cultivates a dynamic and emotionally engaged relationship with the Creator.

4. The Transformative Role of Sufi Practices

Practices such as **dhikr** (remembrance of Allah), **muraqaba** (spiritual meditation), and engaging with a spiritual guide or *murshid* are central to the Sufi path. These methods focus on transcending the limitations of worldly distractions and achieving an elevated state of awareness. By internalizing religious observance, the seeker moves beyond ritualistic formalism toward a more vibrant and intuitive expression of faith. Sufi poetry, metaphors, and symbolic language serve to articulate the ineffable realities encountered on this path and inspire ongoing personal growth.

5. Harmonizing Legalistic Discipline and Spiritual Flexibility

Tasawwuf does not reject the foundations of fiqh and aqeedah; instead, it seeks to perfect them by aligning external practices with internal states. Jurists and spiritual masters alike have emphasized that true submission to Allah demands both adherence to the law and the cultivation of a sincere heart. When legal rulings are enacted with the intention of achieving spiritual purity, they become a means of nurturing both ethical behavior and inner peace. This harmonization ensures that law does not become a mechanical exercise but remains a living force within a dynamic and conscious life.

6. The Impact on Community and Individual Identity

The inner transformation promoted by Tasawwuf resonates on both individual and communal levels. For the individual, personal enlightenment and moral refinement foster resilience and clarity in facing life's challenges. Within the community, a collective emphasis on spiritual well-being nurtures solidarity, empathy, and mutual support. As Muslims strive to embody the principles of justice, mercy, and sincerity, the Sufi emphasis on the heart serves as a counterbalance to legalistic rigidity, ensuring that social relations and communal obligations are underscored by compassion and understanding.

7. Tasawwuf as a Catalyst for Renewal in Islamic Thought

Modern reinterpretations of Islamic thought often draw on Sufi insights to address contemporary challenges such as materialism, fragmentation, and spiritual disenchantment. By revisiting classical teachings with fresh perspectives, some scholars and reformists advocate for an Islam that is as much a heart-based faith as it is a legal tradition. This renewed focus on the inner dimensions invites a broader, more inclusive understanding of religious identity and offers avenues for interfaith dialogue centered on shared values of compassion and truth.

Chapter 32: Reconciling Fiqh and Aqeedah in Daily Life

Islamic life is an intricate tapestry woven from the threads of both *Fiqh*—the detailed rulings governing actions—and *Aqeedah*—the foundational beliefs that shape the worldview. While these two disciplines may appear distinct, their interplay forms the bedrock of a holistic Muslim existence. Understanding how to reconcile fiqh's external regulations with aqeedah's internal convictions is crucial for living Islam authentically in everyday contexts.

1. The Symbiotic Relationship Between Belief and Practice

At its core, Islam insists that belief without action is incomplete, just as ritual acts without proper intention lack value. *Aqeedah* informs the heart's conviction in divine unity, prophecy, and the unseen, which in turn motivates adherence to fiqh's prescriptions. This interdependence means that daily acts of worship, social interactions, and ethical decisions must be rooted in sincere belief. Without this foundation, fiqh risks devolving into empty formalism; conversely, aqeedah without practical application remains theoretical.

2. Intentionality: The Key to Unified Living

The Prophet (pbuh) emphasized *niyyah*—intention—as the linchpin connecting inner faith and outward deeds. Each action, from the mundane to the sacred, gains spiritual weight when accompanied by conscious awareness of Allah. Whether performing prayers, business transactions, or interpersonal dealings, grounding behavior in sincere intention brings fiqh rulings to life, reflecting the believer's aqeedah. This fusion turns obedience into a lived experience of devotion rather than mere compliance.

3. Navigating Complexities and Ambiguities

Daily life presents situations not explicitly covered by classical texts, requiring Muslims to navigate gray areas with wisdom. Here, understanding the objectives of Shariah (*maqasid al-shariah*)—such as the preservation of faith, life, intellect, and dignity—guides decision-making. When legal rulings seem rigid, the principles behind them illuminate flexible, context-sensitive applications that maintain fidelity to both law and belief. This approach fosters a dynamic balance rather than rigid dichotomy.

4. Ethics as a Bridge Between Doctrine and Action

Islamic ethics function as the practical embodiment of aqeedah, serving as a bridge to fiqh rulings. Honesty, justice, patience, and compassion emerge from theological convictions and shape concrete behaviors, from financial honesty to conflict resolution. By cultivating moral virtues, individuals naturally align their actions with the spirit of divine law, preventing dissonance between creed and conduct.

5. Challenges of Modernity and Social Pressures

Modern environments introduce challenges such as secular norms, cultural pluralism, and technological distractions that can strain this reconciliation. For example, navigating social media demands ethical mindfulness rooted in both belief and jurisprudential awareness to avoid harmful speech or falsehood. Similarly, balancing professional obligations with Islamic principles requires thoughtful integration of fiqh rulings within contemporary frameworks, ensuring that faith neither alienates nor is diluted.

6. The Role of Education and Community Support

Sustaining this integration necessitates continuous learning and community engagement. Islamic education that equally emphasizes belief and law equips individuals to apply principles holistically. Moreover, communal environments that foster dialogue, mutual accountability, and shared experiences help maintain coherence between aqeedah and fiqh. Such support systems serve as living laboratories where theory is tested and refined through practice.

7. Spirituality as the Living Heart of Law

Ultimately, spirituality breathes life into legal observance. When fiqh becomes a pathway to cultivating love, reliance, and consciousness of Allah, it transcends mechanical compliance. This spiritual dimension ensures that external observance nurtures inner transformation, making every act an expression of faith. Thus, reconciliation is not merely intellectual but existential, harmonizing the believer's outward form with their inward reality.

Chapter 33: Towards a Revival: The Future of Islamic Creed and Law

The contemporary Muslim world stands at a crossroads where tradition meets unprecedented global challenges and opportunities. The future of *Aqeedah* (Islamic creed) and *Fiqh* (Islamic jurisprudence) hinges on a revival that is both rooted in classical authenticity and responsive to the realities of modern life. This chapter explores the prospects, methods, and obstacles involved in revitalizing Islamic belief and legal practice for coming generations.

1. Reconnecting with Classical Foundations

A genuine revival begins with a return to the rich intellectual heritage of Islam. Renewed study and appreciation of the Quran, Sunnah, and early scholarly works provide a firm foundation from which contemporary Muslims can engage present issues. This does not imply a static replication of the past but rather a dynamic engagement with the sources, preserving their spirit and methodology while addressing new contexts.

2. Embracing Ijtihad for Contextual Relevance

The principle of *ijtihad*—independent reasoning—is indispensable for Islamic law to remain vibrant. Future developments will depend on qualified scholars who can interpret texts in light of evolving social, technological, and ethical landscapes. Ijtihad ensures that fiqh remains a living tradition, adaptable yet anchored in divine guidance, capable of offering solutions for contemporary dilemmas without compromising core principles.

3. Balancing Universality and Diversity

Islamic creed and law have always manifested in diverse cultural and intellectual environments. The revival must respect this plurality, allowing for contextual variations in fiqh while maintaining unity in aqeedah. Such balance fosters inclusivity, avoids sectarian rigidity, and honors the richness of Islamic civilization's global heritage.

4. Integrating Science and Technology

The acceleration of scientific discovery and technological innovation invites a reassessment of traditional rulings and beliefs. Engaging with these advancements critically and thoughtfully can enrich Islamic scholarship. Areas such as bioethics, environmental stewardship, artificial intelligence, and medical jurisprudence will require deep collaboration between religious scholars and experts to develop nuanced, principled responses.

5. Education as a Catalyst for Renewal

Comprehensive educational reforms are pivotal for the revival. Curricula that integrate classical knowledge with contemporary disciplines, foster critical thinking, and encourage ethical reflection will cultivate a generation capable of embodying Islamic values in diverse spheres. Both formal institutions and grassroots learning networks play vital roles in this transformation.

6. Addressing Modern Social Challenges

The revival must confront issues such as gender justice, minority rights, political governance, and global ethics. Islamic law and creed possess profound resources for justice and human dignity, yet these must be articulated clearly and compassionately within modern frameworks. This engagement will not only strengthen Muslim communities but also contribute meaningfully to global moral discourse.

7. The Role of Spiritual Renewal

No revival of creed and law can be complete without a parallel awakening of the spiritual dimension. Revitalizing the inner life through practices of remembrance, reflection, and ethical self-purification nourishes sincerity and resilience. This spiritual grounding ensures that legal and theological renewal transcends mere intellectual exercise and transforms lived reality.

8. Globalization and Interfaith Engagement

In an interconnected world, Muslims interact with diverse cultures and religions more than ever before. Future renewal involves open, respectful dialogue that affirms Islamic identity while seeking common ethical grounds. Such engagement fosters mutual understanding, counters stereotypes, and positions Islam as a constructive participant in global civilization.

9. Overcoming Obstacles to Revival

Challenges to this revival include political instability, ideological polarization, educational gaps, and the co-option of religious discourse for sectarian or extremist ends. Addressing these requires collective will, visionary leadership, and community solidarity. Transparency, intellectual humility, and inclusivity will be critical in navigating these obstacles.

10. Vision for the Future

The future of Islamic creed and law lies in harmonizing timeless truths with present realities, nurturing a faith that is intellectually robust, spiritually alive, and socially relevant. Such a revival promises not only to preserve the identity of Muslim communities but also to enrich the broader human quest for meaning, justice, and peace.

www.ingramcontent.com/pod-product-compliance
Lightning Source LLC
LaVergne TN
LVHW090413210926
848480LV00002B/553